Cats

A LITERARY ANTHOLOGY

Cats

A LITERARY ANTHOLOGY

Edited by Carolyn M. Jones

The British Library

Contents

60 **Cat Tales**

118 Kitten

House Cat

---

*For every house is incomplete without him
and a blessing is lacking in the spirit.*

Christopher Smart

A Perfect Home

The scene of this chronicle is the town of Dawson's Landing, on the Missouri side of the Mississippi, half a day's journey, per steamboat, below St. Louis.

In 1830 it was a snug little collection of modest one and two-story frame dwellings … Each of these pretty homes had a garden in front fenced with white palings, and opulently stocked with hollyhocks, marigolds, touch-me-nots, prince's-feathers and other old-fashioned flowers; while on the window-sills of the houses stood wooden boxes containing moss-rose plants and terra-cotta pots in which grew a breed of geranium whose spread of intensely red blossoms accented the prevailing pink tint of the rose-clad house-front like an explosion of flame. When there was room on the ledge outside of the pots and boxes for a cat, the cat was there – in sunny weather – stretched at full length, asleep and blissful, with her furry belly to the sun and a paw curved over her nose. Then that house was complete, and its contentment and peace were made manifest to the world by this symbol, whose testimony is infallible. A home without a cat – and a well-fed, well-petted and properly revered cat – may be a perfect home, perhaps, but how can it prove title?

Michel Eyquem Montaigne

from *Essais* II xii

Quand je me jouë à ma chatte, qui scait, si elle passe son temps de
moy plus que je ne fay d'elle? … Si j'ay mon heure de commencer
ou de refuser, aussi a elle la sienne.
(When I play with my cat, who knows whether she is diverting
herself with me, more than I with her? … If I have my time to
begin or to refuse, she too has hers.)

Eleanor Farjeon

Cats Sleep Anywhere

Cats sleep anywhere,
Any table, any chair,
Top of piano,
Window-ledge,
In the middle,
On the edge,
Open drawer,
Empty shoe,
Anybody's lap will do,
Fitted in a cardboard box,
In the cupboard
With your frocks–
Anywhere.
They don't care!
Cats sleep anywhere.

Charles Dickens, from *David Copperfield*

Room to Swing a Cat

Mrs Crupp had indignantly assured him that there wasn't room to swing a cat there; but, as Mr. Dick justly observed to me, sitting down on the foot of the bed, nursing his leg, 'You know, Trotwood, I don't want to swing a cat. I never do swing a cat. Therefore, what does that signify to *me!*'

Lewis Carroll, from *A Tangled Tale*

Eligible Apartments

'Does the window open?' was always Balbus' first question in testing
a lodging: and 'Does the chimney smoke?' his second.

* * *

The usual questions were answered satisfactorily: but this time
Hugh added one of his own invention – 'Does the cat scratch?'

The landlady looked round suspiciously, as if to make sure the
cat was not listening. 'I will not deceive you, gentlemen,' she said.
'It do scratch, but not without you pulls its whiskers! It'll never
do it,' she repeated slowly, with a visible effort to recall the exact
words of some written agreement between herself and the cat,
'without you pulls its whiskers!'

'Much may be excused in a cat so treated,' said Balbus, as they
left the house and crossed to Number Seventy-Three, leaving the
landlady curtseying on the doorstep, and still murmuring to herself
her parting words, as if they were a form of blessing, '– not without
you pulls its whiskers!'

Ford Madox Ford

from 'The House'

The Cat of the House. I muse
Over the hearth with my 'minishing eyes
Until after
The last coal dies.
Every tunnel of the mouse,
Every channel of the cricket,
I have smelt.
I have felt
The secret shifting of the mouldered rafter,
And heard
Every bird in the thicket.
I see
You
Nightingale up in the tree.
The Nightingale. The night takes a turn towards coldness; the stars
Waver and shake.
Truly more wake,
More thoughts are afloat;
More folk are afoot than I knew!
The Milch-Goat. I, even I, am the Goat!
The Cat of the House. Enough of your stuff of dust and of mud!
I born of a race of strange things,
Of deserts, great temples, great kings,
In the hot sands where the nightingale never sings!
Old he-gods of ingle and hearth,
Young she-gods of fur and of silk –
Not the mud of the earth –
Are the things that I dream of!

TABLEAUX PARISIENS

Charles Baudelaire

Le Chat

Viens, mon beau chat, sur mon
  cœur amoureux;
Retiens les griffes de ta patte,
Et laisse moi plonger dans tes beaux yeux,
Mêlés de métal et d'agate.

Lorsque mes doigts caressent à loisir
Ta tête et ton dos élastique,
Et que ma main s'enivre du plaisir
Du palper ton corps électrique,

Je vois ma femme en esprit. Son regard,
Comme le tien, amiable bête,
Profond et froid, coupe et fend
  comme un dard,

Et, des pieds jusques à la tête,
Un air subtil, un dangereux parfum,
Nagent autour de son corps brun.

Elizabeth Bishop

Lullaby for the Cat

Minnow, go to sleep and dream,
    Close your great big eyes;
Round your bed Events prepare
    The pleasantest surprise.

Darling Minnow, drop that frown,
    Just cooperate,
Not a kitten shall be drowned
    In the Marxist State.

Joy and Love will both be yours,
    Minnow, don't be glum.
Happy days are coming soon –
    Sleep, and let them come …

Daniel Defoe

from *Robinson Crusoe*

I found also that the island I was in was barren, and, as I saw good
reason to believe, uninhabited except by wild beasts … there sat
a creature like a wild cat upon one of the chests, which, when I
came towards it, ran away a little distance, and then stood still.
She sat very composed and unconcerned, and looked full in my
face, as if she had a mind to be acquainted with me. I presented
my gun at her, but as she did not understand it, she was perfectly
unconcerned at it, nor did she offer to stir away; upon which I
tossed her a bit of biscuit, though, by the way, I was not very

free of it, for my store was not great; however, I spared her a bit,
I say, and she went to it, smelled at it and ate it, and looked (as if
pleased) for more; but I thanked her, and could spare no more, so
she marched off.

* * *

I must not forget that we had in the ship a dog and two cats, of
whose eminent history I may have occasion to say something in
its place; for I carried both the cats with me; and as for the dog, he
jumped out of the ship of himself and swam on shore to me the day
after I went on shore.

* * *

It would have made a Stoic smile to have seen me and my little
family sit down to dinner. There was my majesty the prince and
lord of the whole island; I had the lives of all my subjects at my
absolute command; I could hang, draw, give liberty, and take it
away, and no rebels among all my subjects. Then, to see how like
a king I dined, too, all alone, attended by my servants! Poll, as if
he had been my favourite, was the only person permitted to talk
to me. My dog, who was now grown old and crazy, and had found
no species to multiply his kind upon, sat always at my right hand;
and two cats, one on one side of the table and one on the other,
expecting now and then a bit from my hand, as a mark of
especial favour.

Walter de la Mare

Puss

Puss loves man's winter fire
Now that the sun so soon
Leaves the hours cold it warmed
In burning June.

She purrs full length before
The heaped-up hissing blaze,
Drowsy in slumber down
Her head she lays.

While he with whom she dwells
Sits snug in his inglenook,
Stretches his legs to the flames
And reads his book.

Algernon Charles Swinburne

To a Cat

Stately, kindly, lordly friend,
Condescend
Here to sit by me, and turn
Glorious eyes that smile and burn,
Golden eyes, love's lustrous meed,
On the golden page I read.
All your wondrous wealth of hair,
Dark and fair,
Silken-shaggy, soft and bright
As the clouds and beams of night
Pays my reverent hand's caress
Back with friendlier gentleness.
Dogs may fawn on all and some
As they come;
You, a friend of loftier mind,
Answer friends alone in kind.
Just your foot upon my hand
Softly bids it understand.

James Boswell

from *The Life of Samuel Johnson*

I never shall forget the indulgence with which he treated Hodge, his cat: for whom he himself used to go out and buy oysters, lest the servants having that trouble should take a dislike to the poor creature. I am, unluckily, one of those who have an antipathy to a cat, so that I am uneasy when in the room with one; and I own, I frequently suffered a good deal from the presence of this same Hodge. I recollect him one day scrambling up Dr. Johnson's breast, apparently with much satisfaction, while my friend smiling and half-whistling, rubbed down his back, and pulled him by the tail; and when I observed he was a fine cat, saying, 'why yes, Sir, but I have had cats whom I liked better than this;' and then as if perceiving Hodge to be out of countenance, adding, 'but he is a very fine cat, a very fine cat indeed.'

This reminds me of the ludicrous account which he gave Mr. Langton, of the despicable state of a young Gentleman of good family. 'Sir, when I heard of him last, he was running about town shooting cats.' And then in a sort of kindly reverie, he bethought himself of his own favourite cat, and said, 'But Hodge shan't be shot; no, no, Hodge shall not be shot.'

Mark Twain, from *Roughing It*

A Wonderful Cat

One of my comrades there – another of those victims of eighteen years of unrequited toil and blighted hopes – was one of the gentlest spirits that ever bore its patient cross in a weary exile: grave and simple Dick Baker, pocket-miner of Dead-House Gulch. – He was forty-six, gray as a rat, earnest, thoughtful, slenderly educated, slouchily dressed and clay-soiled, but his heart was finer metal than any gold his shovel ever brought to light – than any, indeed, that ever was mined or minted.

Whenever he was out of luck and a little down-hearted, he would fall to mourning over the loss of a wonderful cat he used to own (for where women and children are not, men of kindly impulses take up with pets, for they must love something). And he always spoke of the strange sagacity of that cat with the air of a man who believed in his secret heart that there was something human about it – may be even supernatural.

I heard him talking about this animal once. He said:

'Gentlemen, I used to have a cat here, by the name of Tom Quartz, which you'd a took an interest in I reckon – most any body would. I had him here eight year – and he was the remarkablest cat I ever see. He was a large gray one of the Tom specie, an' he had more hard, natchral sense than any man in this camp – 'n' a power of dignity – he wouldn't let the Gov'ner of Californy be familiar with him. He never ketched a rat in his life – 'peared to be above it. He never cared for nothing but mining. He knowed more about mining, that cat did, than any man I ever, ever see. You couldn't tell him noth'n 'bout placer diggin's – 'n' as for pocket mining, why he was just born for it. He would dig out after me an' Jim when

we went over the hills prospect'n', and he would trot along behind
us for as much as five mile, if we went so fur. An' he had the best
judgment about mining ground – why you never see anything
like it. When we went to work, he'd scatter a glance around, 'n' if
he didn't think much of the indications, he would give a look as
much as to say, 'Well, I'll have to get you to excuse me,' 'n' without
another word he'd hyste his nose into the air 'n' shove for home.
But if the ground suited him, he would lay low 'n' keep dark till
the first pan was washed, 'n' then he would sidle up 'n' take a look,
an' if there was about six or seven grains of gold he was satisfied
– he didn't want no better prospect 'n' that – 'n' then he would lay
down on our coats and snore like a steamboat till we'd struck the
pocket, an' then get up 'n' superintend. He was nearly lightnin' on
superintending.

'Well, bye an' bye, up comes this yer quartz excitement. Every
body was into it – every body was pick'n' 'n' blast'n' instead of
shovelin' dirt on the hill side – every body was put'n' down a shaft
instead of scrapin' the surface. Noth'n' would do Jim, but we must
tackle the ledges, too, 'n' so we did. We commenced put'n' down
a shaft, 'n' Tom Quartz he begin to wonder what in the Dickens
it was all about. He hadn't ever seen any mining like that before,
'n' he was all upset, as you may say – he couldn't come to a right
understanding of it no way – it was too many for him. He was
down on it, too, you bet you – he was down on it powerful – 'n'
always appeared to consider it the cussedest foolishness out. But
that cat, you know, was always agin new fangled arrangements –
somehow he never could abide 'em. You know how it is with old
habits. But by an' by Tom Quartz begin to git sort of reconciled
a little, though he never could altogether understand that eternal
sinkin' of a shaft an' never pannin' out any thing. At last he got to
comin' down in the shaft, hisself, to try to cipher it out. An' when

he'd git the blues, 'n' feel kind o' scruffy, 'n' aggravated 'n' disgusted
– knowin' as he did, that the bills was runnin' up all the time an'
we warn't makin' a cent – he would curl up on a gunny sack in the
corner an' go to sleep. Well, one day when the shaft was down
about eight foot, the rock got so hard that we had to put in a blast
– the first blast'n' we'd ever done since Tom Quartz was born. An'
then we lit the fuse 'n' clumb out 'n' got off 'bout fifty yards – 'n'

forgot 'n' left Tom Quartz sound asleep on the gunny sack. In 'bout
a minute we seen a puff of smoke bust up out of the hole, 'n' then
everything let go with an awful crash, 'n' about four million ton of
rocks 'n' dirt 'n' smoke 'n' splinters shot up 'bout a mile an' a half
into the air, an' by George, right in the dead centre of it was old
Tom Quartz a goin' end over end, an' a snortin' an' a sneez'n', an' a
clawin' an' a reachin' for things like all possessed. But it warn't no
use, you know, it warn't no use. An' that was the last we see of him
for about two minutes 'n' a half, an' then all of a sudden it begin
to rain rocks and rubbage, an' directly he come down ker-whop
about ten foot off f'm where we stood. Well, I reckon he was p'raps
the orneriest lookin' beast you ever see. One ear was sot back on
his neck, 'n' his tail was stove up, 'n' his eye-winkers was swinged
off, 'n' he was all blacked up with powder an' smoke, an' all sloppy
with mud 'n' slush f'm one end to the other. Well sir, it warn't no
use to try to apologize – we couldn't say a word. He took a sort
of a disgusted look at hisself, 'n' then he looked at us – an' it was
just exactly the same as if he had said – "Gents, may be you think
it's smart to take advantage of a cat that ain't had no experience of
quartz minin', but I think different" – an' then he turned on his heel
'n' marched off home without ever saying another word.

'That was jest his style. An' may be you won't believe it, but
after that you never see a cat so prejudiced agin quartz mining as
what he was. An' by an' bye when he did get to goin' down in the
shaft agin, you'd 'a been astonished at his sagacity. The minute
we'd tetch off a blast 'n' the fuse'd begin to sizzle, he'd give a look
as much as to say: 'Well, I'll have to git you to excuse me,' an' it
was surpris'n' the way he'd shin out of that hole 'n' go f'r a tree.
Sagacity? It ain't no name for it. 'Twas inspiration!'

Christopher Smart

from 'Jubilate Agno'

For I will consider my Cat Jeoffrey.
For he is the servant of the Living God, duly and daily serving him.
For at the First glance of the glory of God in the East he worships
    in his way.
For this is done by wreathing his body seven times round with
    elegant quickness.
For then he leaps up to catch the musk, which is the blessing of
    God upon his prayer.
For he rolls upon prank to work it in.
For having done duty and received blessing he
    begins to consider himself.
For this he performs in ten degrees.
For first he looks upon his fore-paws to see if
    they are clean.
For secondly he kicks up behind to clear
    away there.
For thirdly he works it upon
    stretch with the fore-paws
    extended.
For fourthly he sharpens his
    paws by wood.
For fifthly he washes himself.
For sixthly he rolls upon
    wash.
For seventhly he fleas
    himself, that he may not be
    interrupted upon the beat.

For eighthly he rubs himself against a post.

For ninthly he looks up for his instructions.

For tenthly he goes in quest of food.

For having consider'd God and himself he will consider his neighbour.

For if he meets another cat he will kiss her in kindness.

For when he takes his prey he plays with it to give it a chance.

For one mouse in seven escapes by his dallying.

For when his day's work is done his business more properly begins.

For he keeps the Lord's watch in the night against the adversary.

How he counteracts the powers of darkness by his electrical skin
    and glaring eyes.

For he counteracts the Devil, who is death, by brisking about the
    life.

For in his morning orisons he loves the sun and the sun loves him.

For he is of the tribe of Tiger.

For the Cherub Cat is a term of the Angel Tiger.

For he has the subtlety and hissing of a serpent, which in goodness
    he suppresses.

For he will not do destruction, if he is well fed, neither will he spit
    without provocation.

For he purrs in thankfulness, when God tells him he's a good Cat.

For he is an instrument for the children to learn benevolence upon.

For every house is incomplete without him and a blessing is lacking
    in the spirit.

For the Lord commanded Moses concerning the cats at the
    departure of the Children of Israel from Egypt.

For every family had one cat at least in the bag.

For the English Cats are the best in Europe.

For he is the cleanest in the use of his fore-paws of any quadruped.

For the dexterity of his defence is an instance of the love of God to
    him exceedingly.

For he is the quickest to his mark of any creature.

For he is tenacious of his point.

For he is a mixture of gravity and waggery.

For he knows that God is his Saviour.

For there is nothing sweeter than his peace when at rest.

For there is nothing brisker than his life when in motion.

For he is of the Lord's poor and so indeed is he called by
    benevolence perpetually – Poor Jeoffrey! poor Jeoffrey! the rat
    has bit thy throat.

For I bless the name of the Lord Jesus that Jeoffrey is better.

For the divine spirit comes about his body to sustain it in
    complete cat.

For his tongue is exceedingly pure so that it has in purity what it
    wants in music.

For he is docile and can learn certain things.

For he can set up with gravity which is patience upon approbation.

For he can fetch and carry, which is patience in employment.

For he can jump over a stick which is patience upon proof positive.

For he can spraggle upon waggle at the word of command.

For he can jump from an eminence into his master's bosom.

For he can catch the cork and toss it again.

For he is hated by the hypocrite and the miser.

For the former is afraid of detection.

For the latter refuses the charge.

For he camels his back to bear the first notion of business.

For he is good to think on, if a man would express himself neatly.

For he made a great figure in Egypt for his signal services.

For he killed the Ichneumon-rat very pernicious by land.

For his ears are so acute that they sting again.

For from this proceeds the passing quickness of his attention.

For by stroking of him I have found out electricity.

For I perceived God's light upon him both wax and fire.
For the Electrical fire is the spiritual substance, which God sends
    from heaven to sustain the bodies of both man and beast.

Attributed to John Greenleaf Whittier

For a Little Girl Mourning her Favorite Cat

Bathsheba:
To whom none ever said scat,
No worthier cat
Ever sat on a mat
Or caught a rat:
Requies-cat.

Hunter

---

*For he is the quickest to his
mark of any creature.*

Christopher Smart

The Worth of Cat

There is a record of protective legislation – sure sign of an animal's practical value – as long ago as the year 948. A prince of South Wales called Hywel the Good, or Hywel Dda, recorded the value of a cat. 'The worth of a kitten, from the night it is kittened until it shall open its eyes, is a legal penny; and from that time until it shall kill mice, twopence. After it shall kill mice, four legal pence.' A cat, it is laid down, must be able 'to see, to hear, to kill mice, and to have her claws' and must be 'Perfect of ear, perfect of teeth, perfect of tail, perfect of slaws, and without marks of fire'. The last phrase can probably be explained by the fact that singed fur would indicate a cat which preferred lying by the fire to catching rats and mice.

The penalty for killing or stealing an animal so useful in the village granaries of those days was 'the worth of cat'. This is defined as follows: 'Its head is to be put downwards upon a clean, even floor, with its tail lifted upwards, and there suspended whilst wheat is poured about it until the tip of its tail be covered, and that is its worth.'

Walter de la Mare

Five Eyes

In Hans' old Mill his three black cats
Watch his bins for the thieving rats.
Whisker and claw, they crouch in the night,
Their five eyes smouldering green and bright:
Squeaks from the flour sacks, squeaks from where
The cold wind stirs on the empty stair,
Squeaking and scampering, everywhere.
Then down they pounce, now in, now out,
At whisking tail, and sniffing snout;
While lean old Hans he snores away
Till peep of light at break of day;
Then up he climbs to his creaking mill,
Out come his cats all grey with meal –
Jekkel, and Jessup, and one-eyed Jill.

John Keats

On Mrs. Reynolds's Cat

Cat! who hast pass'd thy grand climacteric,
How many mice and rats hast in thy days
Destroy'd? How many tit bits stolen? Gaze
With those bright languid segments green, and prick
Those velvet ears – but pr'ythee do not stick
Thy latent talons in me – and upraise
Thy gentle mew – and tell me all thy frays
Of fish and mice, and rats and tender chick.
Nay, look not down, nor lick thy dainty wrists –
For all thy wheezy asthma, – and for all
Thy tail's tip is nicked off – and though the fists
Of many a maid have given thee many a maul,
Still is that fur as soft as when the lists
In youth thou enter'dst on glass-bottled wall.

Richard Adams, from *Watership Down*

A Good Rabbit's a Match
for a Cat, Any Day

Suddenly Pipkin spoke from the floor. 'Hazel, there's a cat in the yard outside!'

'We're not afraid of cats,' said Hazel to Boxwood, 'as long as we're in the open.' Trying to appear unhurried, he went back to the floor by way of the straw-bale and crossed over to the door. Pipkin was looking through the hinge. He was plainly frightened.

'I think it's smelt us, Hazel,' he said. 'I'm afraid it knows where we are.'

'Don't stay there, then,' said Hazel. 'Follow me close and run when I do.' Without waiting to look out through the hinge, he went round the half-open door of the shed and stopped on the threshold.

The cat, a tabby with white chest and paws, was at the farther end of the little yard, walking slowly and deliberately along the side of a pile of logs. When Hazel appeared in the doorway it saw him at once and stood stock-still, with staring eyes and twitching tail. Hazel hopped slowly across the threshold and stopped again. Already sunlight was slanting across the yard and in the stillness the flies buzzed about a patch of dung a few feet away. There was a smell of straw and dust and hawthorn.

'You look hungry,' said Hazel to the cat. 'Rats getting too clever, I suppose?'

The cat made no reply. Hazel sat blinking in the sunshine. The cat crouched almost flat on the ground, thrusting its head forward between its front paws. Close behind, Pipkin fidgeted and Hazel, never taking his eyes from the cat, could sense that he was trembling.

'Don't be frightened, Hlao-roo,' he whispered. 'I'll get you away, but you must wait till it comes for us. Keep still.'

The cat began to lash its tail. Its hindquarters lifted and wagged from side to side in mounting excitement.

'Can you run?' said Hazel. 'I think not. Why, you pop-eyed, back-door saucer-scraper –'

The cat flung itself across the yard and the two rabbits leapt into flight with great thrusts of their hind legs. The cat came very fast indeed and although both of them had been braced ready to move on the instant, they were barely out of the yard in time. Racing up the side of the long barn, they heard the Labrador barking in excitement as it ran to the full extent of its rope. A man's voice shouted to it. From the cover of the hedge beside the lane they turned and looked back. The cat had stopped short and was licking one paw with a pretence of nonchalance.

'They hate to look silly,' said Hazel. 'It won't give us any more trouble.'

* * *

'What annoys me,' [said Bigwig], 'is to think that you ran from that cat. A good rabbit's a match for a cat, any day. My mother went for one once and she fairly gave it something to remember, I can tell you: scratched its fur out like willowherb in autumn! Just leave the farm cats to me and one or two of the others!'

* * *

Bigwig's hopes of action were fulfilled almost at once. The cat that he met as he reached the far end of the barn was not Hazel's tabby, but another; ginger, black and white (and therefore a female); one of those slim, trotting, quick-moving, tail-twitching cats that sit on farm window-sills in the rain or keep watch from the tops of sacks on sunny afternoons. It came briskly round the corner of the barn, saw the rabbits and stopped dead.

Without an instant's hesitation Bigwig went straight for it, as though it had been the beech branch on the down. But quicker even than he Dandelion ran forward, scratched it and leapt clear. As it turned, Bigwig threw his full weight upon it from the other side. The cat closed with him, biting and scratching, and Bigwig rolled over on the ground. The others could hear him swearing like a cat himself and struggling for a hold. Then he sank one back leg into the cat's side and kicked backwards rapidly, several times.

Anyone who is familiar with cats knows that they do not care for a determined assailant. A dog that tries to make itself pleasant to a cat may very well get scratched for its pains. But let that same dog rush in to the attack and many a cat will not wait to meet it. The farm cat was bewildered by the speed and fury of Bigwig's charge. It was no weakling and a good ratter, but it had the bad luck to be up against a dedicated fighter who was spoiling for action. As it scrabbled out of Bigwig's reach, Speedwell cuffed it across the face. This was the last blow struck, for the wounded cat made off across the yard and disappeared under the fence of the cow-byre.

Anon, translated from the Yoruba by Ulli Beier

Leopard

Gentle hunter
his tail plays on the ground
While he crushes the skull.

Beautiful death
who puts on a spotted robe
when he goes to his victim.

Playful killer
whose loving embrace
splits the antelope's heart.

Charlotte Brontë, from *Villette*

Like a Cat

Behold Madame, in shawl, wrapping-gown and slippers, softly
descending the steps, and stealing like a cat round the garden: in
two minutes she would have been upon Dr. John. If *she* were like a
cat, however, *he* quite as much resembled a leopard: nothing could
be lighter than his tread when he chose. He watched, and as she
turned a corner, he took the garden at two noiseless bounds.
She reappeared, and he was gone.

Geoffrey Chaucer, from *The Canterbury Tales*

from 'The Manciple's Tale'

Lat take a cat, and fostre hym wel with milk,
And tendre flessh, and make his couche of silk,
And lat hym seen a mous go by the wal;
Anon he weyveth[1] milk, and flessh, and al,
And every deyntee that is in the hous,
Swich appetyt hath he to ete a mous.

---

1 Abandons

Matthew Arnold

from 'Poor Matthias'

Poor Matthias! Wouldst thou have
More than pity? claim'st a stave?
– Friends more near us than a bird
We dismiss'd without a word.
Rover, with the good brown head,
Great Atossa, they are dead;
Dead, and neither prose nor rhyme
Tells the praises of their prime.
Thou didst know them old and grey,
Know them in their sad decay.
Thou hast seen Atossa sage
Sit for hours beside thy cage;
Thou wouldst chirp, thou foolish bird,
Flutter, chirp – she never stirr'd!
What were now these toys to her?
Down she sank amid her fur;
Eyed thee with a soul resign'd –
And thou deemedst cats were kind!
– Cruel, but composed and bland,
Dumb, inscrutable and grand,
So Tiberius might have sat,
Had Tiberius been a cat.

A Web of Complex Relations

I am tempted to give one more instance showing how plants and
animals, most remote in the scale of nature, are bound together
by a web of complex relations … From experiments which I have
tried, I have found that the visits of bees, if not indispensable, are
at least highly beneficial to the fertilisation of our clovers; but
humble-bees alone visit the common red clover (*Trifolium pratense*),
as other bees cannot reach the nectar. Hence I have very little
doubt, that if the whole genus of humble-bees became extinct or
very rare in England, the heartsease and red clover would become
very rare, or wholly disappear. The number of humble-bees in any
district depends in a great degree on the number of field-mice,
which destroy their combs and nests; and Mr. H. Newman, who
has long attended to the habits of humble-bees, believes that 'more
than two-thirds of them are thus destroyed all over England'. Now
the number of mice is largely dependent, as every one knows, on
the number of cats; and Mr. Newman says, 'Near villages and small
towns I have found the nests of humble-bees more numerous than
elsewhere, which I attribute to the number of cats that destroy
the mice.' Hence it is quite credible that the presence of a feline
animal in large numbers in a district might determine, through the
intervention first of mice and then of bees, the frequency of certain
flowers in that district!

Gilbert White, from *The Natural History of Selborne*

Their Violent Fondness for Fish

There is a propensity belonging to common house-cats that is very remarkable; I mean their violent fondness for fish, which appears to be their most favourite food: and yet nature in this instance seems to have planted in them an appetite that, unassisted, they know not how to gratify: for of all quadrupeds cats are the least disposed towards water; and will not, when they can avoid it, deign to wet a foot, much less to plunge into that element.

Thomas Gray

On a Favourite Cat, Drowned in a Tub of Fishes

'Twas on a lofty vase's side,
Where China's gayest art had dyed
The azure flowers that blow;
Demurest of the tabby kind
The pensive Selima reclined,
Gazed on the lake below.

Her conscious tail her joy declared;
The fair round face, the snowy beard,
The velvet of her paws,
Her coat that with the tortoise vies,
Her ears of jet, and emerald eyes,

She saw; and purr'd applause.
Still had she gazed; but 'midst the tide
Two angel forms were seen to glide,
The Genii of the stream:
Their scaly armour's Tyrian hue
Through richest purple, to the view
Betrayed a golden gleam.

The hapless Nymph with wonder saw:
A whisker first, and then a claw,
With many an ardent wish,
She stretch'd, in vain, to reach the prize —
What female heart can gold despise?
What Cat's averse to Fish?

Presumptuous maid! with looks intent
Again she stretch'd, again she bent,
Nor knew the gulf between —
Malignant Fate sat by, and smiled —
The slippery verge her feet beguiled;
She tumbled headlong in!

Eight times emerging from the flood
She mew'd to every watery God
Some speedy aid to send: —
No Dolphin came, no Nereid stirr'd:
Nor cruel Tom, nor Susan heard.
A favourite has no friend!

From hence, ye Beauties! undeceived,
Know one false step is ne'er retrieved,
And be with caution bold:
Not all that tempts your wandering eyes
And heedless hearts, is lawful prize;
Nor all that glisters, gold.

O. Henry

The Princess and the Puma

There had to be a king and queen, of course. The king was a
terrible old man who wore six-shooters and spurs, and shouted in
such a tremendous voice that the rattlers on the prairie would run
into their holes under the prickly pear. Before there was a royal
family they called the man 'Whispering Ben'. When he came to
own 50,000 acres of land and more cattle than he could count, they
called him O'Donnell 'the Cattle King'.

The queen had been a Mexican girl from Laredo. She made a
good, mild, Colorado-claro wife, and even succeeded in teaching
Ben to modify his voice sufficiently while in the house to keep the
dishes from being broken. When Ben got to be king she would
sit on the gallery of Espinosa Ranch and weave rush mats. When
wealth became so irresistible and oppressive that upholstered chairs
and a centre table were brought down from San Antone in the
wagons, she bowed her smooth, dark head, and shared the fate
of the Danae.

To avoid lèse-majesté you have been presented first to the king
and queen. They do not enter the story, which might be called
'The Chronicle of the Princess, the Happy Thought, and the Lion
that Bungled his Job'.

Josefa O'Donnell was the surviving daughter, the princess.
From her mother she inherited warmth of nature and a dusky,
semi-tropic beauty. From Ben O'Donnell the royal she acquired
a store of intrepidity, common sense and the faculty of ruling.
The combination was one worth going miles to see. Josefa while
riding her pony at a gallop could put five out of six bullets through
a tomato-can swinging at the end of a string. She could play for

hours with a white kitten she owned, dressing it in all manner of absurd clothes. Scorning a pencil, she could tell you out of her head what 1545 two-year-olds would bring on the hoof, at $8.50 per head. Roughly speaking, the Espinosa Ranch is forty miles long and thirty broad – but mostly leased land. Josefa, on her pony, had prospected over every mile of it. Every cow-puncher on the range knew her by sight and was a loyal vassal. Ripley Givens, foreman of one of the Espinosa outfits, saw her one day, and made up his mind to form a royal matrimonial alliance. Presumptuous? No. In those days in the Nueces country a man was a man. And, after all, the title of cattle king does not presuppose blood royalty. Often it only signifies that its owner wears the crown in token of his magnificent qualities in the art of cattle stealing.

One day Ripley Givens rode over to the Double Elm Ranch to inquire about a bunch of strayed yearlings. He was late in setting out on his return trip, and it was sundown when he struck the White Horse Crossing of the Nueces. From there to his own camp it was sixteen miles. To the Espinosa ranch it was twelve. Givens was tired. He decided to pass the night at the Crossing.

There was a fine water hole in the river-bed. The banks were thickly covered with great trees, undergrown with brush. Back from the water hole fifty yards was a stretch of curly mesquite grass – supper for his horse and bed for himself. Givens staked his horse, and spread out his saddle blankets to dry. He sat down with his back against a tree and rolled a cigarette. From somewhere in the dense timber along the river came a sudden, rageful, shivering wail. The pony danced at the end of his rope and blew a whistling snort of comprehending fear. Givens puffed at his cigarette, but he reached leisurely for his pistol-belt, which lay on the grass, and twirled the cylinder of his weapon tentatively. A great gar plunged with a loud splash into the water hole. A little brown rabbit skipped around a bunch of catclaw and sat twitching his whiskers and looking humorously at Givens. The pony went on eating grass.

It is well to be reasonably watchful when a Mexican lion sings soprano along the arroyos at sundown. The burden of his song may be that young calves and fat lambs are scarce, and that he has a carnivorous desire for your acquaintance.

In the grass lay an empty fruit can, cast there by some former sojourner. Givens caught sight of it with a grunt of satisfaction. In his coat pocket tied behind his saddle was a handful or two of ground coffee. Black coffee and cigarettes! What ranchero could desire more?

In two minutes he had a little fire going clearly. He started, with his can, for the water hole. When within fifteen yards of its edge he saw, between the bushes, a side-saddled pony with down-dropped reins cropping grass a little distance to his left. Just rising from her hands and knees on the brink of the water hole was Josefa O'Donnell. She had been drinking water, and she brushed the sand from the palms of her hands. Ten yards away, to her right, half concealed by a clump of sacuista, Givens saw the crouching form of the Mexican lion. His amber eyeballs glared hungrily; six feet from them was the tip of the tail stretched straight, like a pointer's. His hind-quarters rocked with the motion of the cat tribe preliminary to leaping.

Givens did what he could. His six-shooter was thirty-five yards away lying on the grass. He gave a loud yell, and dashed between the lion and the princess.

The 'ruckus,' as Givens called it afterward, was brief and somewhat confused. When he arrived on the line of attack he saw a dim streak in the air, and heard a couple of faint cracks. Then a hundred pounds of Mexican lion plumped down upon his head and flattened him, with a heavy jar, to the ground. He remembered calling out: 'Let up, now – no fair gouging!' and then he crawled from under the lion like a worm, with his mouth full of grass and dirt, and a big lump on the back of his head where it had struck the root of a water-elm. The lion lay motionless. Givens, feeling aggrieved, and suspicious of fouls, shook his fist at the lion, and shouted: 'I'll rastle you again for twenty – ' and then he got back to himself.

Josefa was standing in her tracks, quietly reloading her silver-mounted .38. It had not been a difficult shot. The lion's head made an easier mark than a tomato-can swinging at the end of a string. There was a provoking, teasing, maddening smile upon her mouth and in her dark eyes. The would-be-rescuing knight felt the fire of his fiasco burn down to his soul. Here had been his chance, the chance that he had dreamed of; and Momus, and not Cupid, had presided over it. The satyrs in the wood were, no doubt, holding their sides in hilarious, silent laughter. There had been something like vaudeville – say Signor Givens and his funny knockabout act with the stuffed lion.

'Is that you, Mr. Givens?' said Josefa, in her deliberate, saccharine contralto. 'You nearly spoilt my shot when you yelled. Did you hurt your head when you fell?'

'Oh, no,' said Givens, quietly; 'that didn't hurt.' He stooped ignominiously and dragged his best Stetson hat from under the beast. It was crushed and wrinkled to a fine comedy effect. Then he knelt down and softly stroked the fierce, open-jawed head of the dead lion.

'Poor old Bill!' he exclaimed mournfully.

'What's that?' asked Josefa, sharply.

'Of course you didn't know, Miss Josefa,' said Givens, with an air of one allowing magnanimity to triumph over grief. 'Nobody can blame you. I tried to save him, but I couldn't let you know in time.'

'Save who?'

'Why, Bill. I've been looking for him all day. You see, he's been our camp pet for two years. Poor old fellow, he wouldn't have hurt a cottontail rabbit. It'll break the boys all up when they hear about it. But you couldn't tell, of course, that Bill was just trying to play with you.'

Josefa's black eyes burned steadily upon him. Ripley Givens met the test successfully. He stood rumpling the yellow-brown curls on his head pensively. In his eye was regret, not unmingled with a gentle reproach. His smooth features were set to a pattern of indisputable sorrow. Josefa wavered.

'What was your pet doing here?' she asked, making a last stand. 'There's no camp near the White Horse Crossing.'

'The old rascal ran away from camp yesterday,' answered Givens readily. 'It's a wonder the coyotes didn't scare him to death. You see, Jim Webster, our horse wrangler, brought a little terrier pup into camp last week. The pup made life miserable for Bill – he used to chase him around and chew his hind legs for hours at a time. Every night when bedtime came Bill would sneak under one of the boy's blankets and sleep to keep the pup from finding him. I reckon he must have been worried pretty desperate or he wouldn't have run away. He was always afraid to get out of sight of camp.'

Josefa looked at the body of the fierce animal. Givens gently patted one of the formidable paws that could have killed a yearling calf with one blow. Slowly a red flush widened upon the dark olive face of the girl. Was it the signal of shame of the true sportsman who has brought down ignoble quarry? Her eyes grew softer, and the lowered lids drove away all their bright mockery.

'I'm very sorry,' she said humbly; 'but he looked so big, and jumped so high that – '

'Poor old Bill was hungry,' interrupted Givens, in quick defence

of the deceased. 'We always made him jump for his supper in camp.
He would lie down and roll over for a piece of meat. When he saw
you he thought he was going to get something to eat from you.'

Suddenly Josefa's eyes opened wide.

'I might have shot you!' she exclaimed. 'You ran right in between.
You risked your life to save your pet! That was fine, Mr. Givens.
I like a man who is kind to animals.'

Yes; there was even admiration in her gaze now. After all, there
was a hero rising out of the ruins of the anti-climax. The look
on Givens's face would have secured him a high position in the
S.P.C.A.

'I always loved 'em,' said he; 'horses, dogs, Mexican lions, cows,
alligators – '

'I hate alligators,' instantly demurred Josefa; 'crawly, muddy
things!'

'Did I say alligators?' said Givens. 'I meant antelopes, of course.'
Josefa's conscience drove her to make further amends. She held out
her hand penitently. There was a bright, unshed drop in each of
her eyes.

'Please forgive me, Mr. Givens, won't you? I'm only a girl, you
know, and I was frightened at first. I'm very, very sorry I shot Bill.
You don't know how ashamed I feel. I wouldn't have done it for
anything.'

Givens took the proffered hand. He held it for a time while he
allowed the generosity of his nature to overcome his grief at the
loss of Bill. At last it was clear that he had forgiven her.

'Please don't speak of it any more, Miss Josefa. 'Twas enough to
frighten any young lady the way Bill looked. I'll explain it all right
to the boys.'

'Are you really sure you don't hate me?' Josefa came closer to him
impulsively. Her eyes were sweet – oh, sweet and pleading with

gracious penitence. 'I would hate anyone who would kill my kitten. And how daring and kind of you to risk being shot when you tried to save him! How very few men would have done that!' Victory wrested from defeat! Vaudeville turned into drama! Bravo, Ripley Givens!

It was now twilight. Of course Miss Josefa could not be allowed to ride on to the ranch-house alone. Givens resaddled his pony in spite of that animal's reproachful glances, and rode with her. Side by side they galloped across the smooth grass, the princess and the man who was kind to animals. The prairie odours of fruitful earth and delicate bloom were thick and sweet around them. Coyotes yelping over there on the hill! No fear. And yet –

Josefa rode closer. A little hand seemed to grope. Givens found it with his own. The ponies kept an even gait. The hands lingered together, and the owner of one explained:

'I never was frightened before, but just think! How terrible it would be to meet a really wild lion! Poor Bill! I'm so glad you came with me!'

O'Donnell was sitting on the ranch gallery.

'Hello, Rip!' he shouted – 'that you?'

'He rode in with me,' said Josefa. 'I lost my way and was late.'

'Much obliged,' called the cattle king. 'Stop over, Rip, and ride to camp in the morning.'

But Givens would not. He would push on to camp. There was a bunch of steers to start off on the trail at daybreak. He said good-night, and trotted away.

An hour later, when the lights were out, Josefa, in her night-robe, came to her door and called to the king in his own room across the brick-paved hallway:

'Say, pop, you know that old Mexican lion they call the 'Gotch-eared Devil' – the one that killed Gonzales, Mr. Martin's sheep

herder, and about fifty calves on the Salado range? Well, I settled
his hash this afternoon over at the White Horse Crossing. Put two
balls in his head with my .38 while he was on the jump. I knew him
by the slice gone from his left ear that old Gonzales cut off with his
machete. You couldn't have made a better shot yourself, daddy.'

'Bully for you!' thundered Whispering Ben from the darkness
of the royal chamber.

The Most Lamentable
and Dreadful Sound

All at once a deep fearful sound echoed through the neighbouring
woods. It made our blood curdle in our veins. We listened with
straining ears, hoping it would not be repeated. With a shudder we
heard the dread voice roar again, yet nearer to us, and an answer
peal from the distance.

* * *

The dogs planted themselves by the fire, gazing fixedly landward,
with ears erect, and occasionally uttering a barking challenge, or a
suppressed howl.

Meantime, the horrid roarings approached nearer, and I
concluded that a couple of leopards or panthers had been attracted
by the scent of the boar's carcase.

But not long after I had expressed this opinion, we beheld a large
powerful animal spring from the underwood, and, with a bound
and muttered roar, approach the fire. In a moment I recognized the

unmistakeable outlines of the form of a lion, though in size he far surpassed any I had ever seen exhibited in Europe.

The dogs slunk behind the fire, and the lion seated himself almost like a cat on his hind legs, glaring alternately at them, and at the great boar hams which hung near, with doubtless a mixed feeling of irritation and appetite, which was testified by the restless movement of his tail.

He then arose, and commenced walking up and down with slow and measured pace, occasionally uttering short, angry roars, quite unlike the prolonged full tones we had heard at first.

At times he went to drink at the brook, always returning with such haste, that I fully expected to see him spring.

Gradually his manner became more and more threatening; he turned towards us, crouched, and with his body at full stretch, waved his tail, and glared so furiously, that I was in doubt whether to fire, or retreat, when through the darkness rang the sharp crack of a rifle.

'That is Fritz!' exclaimed everyone; while, with a fearful roar, the lion sprang to his feet, stood stock still, tottered, sank on his knees, rolled over, and lay motionless on the sand.

'We are saved!' I cried; 'that was a masterly shot. The lion is struck to the heart: he will never stir again. Stay on board, boys. I must join my brave Fritz.'

In a few moments I landed: the dogs met me with evident tokens of pleasure, but kept whining uneasily, and looking towards the deep darkness of the wood whence the lion had come.

This behaviour made me cautious; and seeing nothing of Fritz, I lingered by the boat, when suddenly a lioness bounded from the shadow of the trees, into the light diffused by the fire.

At sight of the blazing faggots she paused, as though startled; passed with uncertain step round the outskirts of the illuminated circle; and uttered roarings, which were evidently calls to her mate, whose dead body she presently discovered.

Finding him motionless, her manner betokened the greatest concern; she touched him with her fore-paws, smelt round him and licked his bleeding wounds. Then raising her head, she gnashed her teeth, and gave forth the most lamentable and dreadful sound I ever heard; a mingled roar and howl, which was like the expression of grief, rage and a vow to be revenged, all in one.

D. H. Lawrence

Mountain Lion

Climbing through the January snow, into the Lobo canyon
Dark grow the spruce-trees, blue is the balsam, water sounds still
    unfrozen, and the trail is still evident

Men!
Two men!
Men! The only animal in the world to fear!

They hesitate.
We hesitate.
They have a gun.
We have no gun.

Then we all advance, to meet.

Two Mexicans, strangers, emerging out of the dark and snow and
    inwardness of the Lobo valley.
What are they doing here on this vanishing trail?
What is he carrying?
Something yellow.
A deer?

Qué tiene amigo?
León —

He smiles, foolishly, as if he were caught doing wrong.
And we smile, foolishly, as if we didn't know.

He is quite gentle and dark-faced.

It is a mountain lion,
A long, long slim cat, yellow like a lioness.
Dead.

He trapped her this morning, he says, smiling foolishly.

Lift up her face,
Her round, bright face, bright as frost.
Her round, fine-fashioned head, with two dead ears;
And stripes in the brilliant frost of her face, sharp, fine dark rays,
Dark, keen, fine rays in the brilliant frost of her face.
Beautiful dead eyes.

Hermoso es!

They go out towards the open;
We go out into the gloom of Lobo.
And above the trees I found her lair,
A hole in the blood-orange brilliant rocks that stick up, little cave.
And bones, and twigs, and a perilous ascent.
So, she will never leap up that way again, with the yellow flash of a
    mountain lion's long shoot!
And her bright striped frost-face will never watch any more, out of
    the shadow of the cave in the blood-orange rock,
Above the trees of the Lobo dark valley-mouth!

Instead, I look out.
And out to the dim of the desert, like a dream, never real;
To the snow of the Sangre de Cristo Mountains, the ice of the
    mountains of Picoris,
And near across at the opposite steep of snow, green trees
    motionless standing in snow, like a Christmas toy.

And I think in this empty world there was room for me and a
    mountain lion.
And I think in the world beyond, how easily we might spare a
    million or two humans
And never miss them.
Yet what a gap in the world, the missing white frost-face of that
    slim yellow mountain lion!

The Monk and his Cat

I and my white Pangur
Have each his special art:
His mind is set on hunting mice,
Mine is upon my special craft.
I love to rest – better than any fame!
With close study at my little book;
White Pangur does not envy me:

He loves his childish play.
When in our house we two are all alone …
A tale without tedium.
We have sport never-ending!
Something to exercise our wit.
At times by feats of derring-do
a mouse sticks in his net,
while into my net there drops
a difficult problem of hard meaning.
He points his full shining eye
against the fence of the wall:
I point my clear though feeble eye
against the keenness of science.
He rejoices with quick leaps
when in his sharp claw sticks a mouse;
I, too, rejoice when I have grasped
a problem difficult and dearly loved.
Though we are thus at all time,
neither hinders the other,
each of us pleased with his own art
amuses himself alone.
He is master of the work
which every day he does:
While I am at my own work
to bring difficulty to clearness.

Cat Tales

For he is good to think on, if a man would express himself neatly.

Christopher Smart

The Elopement of the Captain's Daughter

Chorus	Carefully on tiptoe stealing
	Breathing gently as we may
	Ev'ry step with caution feeling
	We will softly steal away.
	Goodness me!
	Why, what was that?
Deadeye	Silent be, it was the cat!
Chorus	It was, it was, it was the cat!
Captain Corcoran	They're right, it was the cat![2]
Chorus	Pull ashore in fashion steady,
	Hymen will defray the fare,
	For a clergyman is ready
	To unite the happy pair.
	Goodness me, why, what was that?
Deadeye	Silent be, again the cat!
Chorus	It was again that cat!

---

2   The would-be bridegroom does not realise that the elopement plan has been betrayed, and the Captain is waiting for him with a different kind of cat – the cat'o'nine tails.

The Cheshire-Cat

Alice was just beginning to think to herself, 'Now, what am I to do with this creature, when I get it home?' when it grunted again, so violently, that she looked down into its face in some alarm. This time there could be no mistake about it: it was neither more or less than a pig, and she felt that it would be quite absurd for her to carry it any further.

So she set the little creature down, and felt quite relieved to see it trot away quietly into the wood. 'If it had grown up,' she said to herself, 'it would have made a dreadfully ugly child: but it makes rather a handsome pig, I think.' And she began thinking over other children she knew, who might do very well as pigs, and was just saying to herself 'if one only knew the right way to change them – ' when she was a little startled by seeing the Cheshire-Cat sitting on a bough of a tree a few yards off.

The Cat only grinned when it saw Alice. It looked good-natured, she thought: still, it had *very* long claws and a great many teeth, so she felt that it ought to be treated with respect.

'Cheshire-Puss,' she began rather timidly, as she did not at all know whether it would like the name: however, it only grinned a little wider. 'Come, it's pleased so far,' thought Alice, and she went on. 'Would you tell me, please, which way I ought to go?'

'That depends a good deal on where you want to get to,' said the Cat.

'I don't much care where – ' said Alice.

'Then it doesn't matter which way you go,' said the Cat.

' – so long as I get *somewhere*,' Alice added as an explanation.

'Oh, you're sure to do that,' said the Cat, 'if you only walk long enough.'

Alice felt that this could not be denied, so she tried another question. 'What sort of people live about here?'

'In *that* direction,' the Cat said, waving its right paw round, 'lives a Hatter: and in *that* direction,' waving the other paw, 'lives a March Hare. Visit either you like: they're both mad.'

'But I don't want to go among mad people,' Alice remarked.

'Oh, you ca'n't help that,' said the Cat: 'we're all mad here. I'm mad. You're mad.'

'How do you know I'm mad?' said Alice.

'You must be,' said the Cat, 'or you wouldn't have come here.'

Alice didn't think that proved it at all: however, she went on: 'And how do you know that you're mad?'

'To begin with,' said the Cat, 'a dog's not mad. You grant that?'

'I suppose so,' said Alice.

'Well, then,' the Cat went on, 'you see a dog growls when it's angry, and wags its tail when it's pleased. Now *I* growl when I'm pleased, and wag my tail when I'm angry. Therefore I'm mad.'

'*I* call it purring, not growling,' said Alice.

'Call it what you like,' said the Cat. 'Do you play croquet with the Queen to-day?'

'I should like it very much,' said Alice, 'but I haven't been invited yet.'

'You'll see me there,' said the Cat, and vanished.

Alice was not much surprised at this, she was getting so well used to queer things happening. While she was still looking at the place it had been, it suddenly appeared again.

'By-the-bye, what became of the baby?' said the Cat. 'I'd nearly forgotten to ask.'

'It turned into a pig,' Alice answered very quietly, just as if the Cat had come back in a natural way.

'I thought it would,' said the Cat, and vanished again.

Alice waited a little, half expecting to see it again, but it did not appear, and after a minute or two she walked on in the direction in which the March Hare was said to live. 'I've seen hatters before,' she said to herself: 'the March Hare will be much the most interesting, and perhaps, as this is May, it wo'n't be raving mad – at least not so mad as it was in March.' As she said this, she looked up, and there was the Cat again, sitting on the branch of a tree.

'Did you say 'pig', or 'fig'?' said the Cat.

'I said 'pig',' replied Alice, 'and I wish you wouldn't keep
appearing and vanishing so suddenly: you make one quite giddy!'

'All right,' said the Cat; and this time it vanished quite slowly,
beginning with the end of the tail, and ending with the grin, which
remained some time after the rest of it had gone.

'Well! I've often seen a cat without a grin,' thought Alice;
'but a grin without a cat! It's the most curious thing I ever saw
in all my life!'

William Shakespeare

from *The Merchant of Venice* Act IV, scene i

Shylock Some men there are love not a gaping pig;
     Some, that are mad if they behold a cat;
     And others, when the bagpipe sings i'the nose,
     Cannot contain their urine: for affection,
     Mistress of passion, sways it to the mood
     Of what it likes, or loathes. Now, for your answer:
     As there is no firm reason to be render'd,

Why he cannot abide a gaping pig;
Why he, a harmless necessary cat;
Why he, a wauling bagpipe; but of force
Must yield to such inevitable shame
As to offend, himself being offended;
So can I give no reason, nor I will not,
More than a lodg'd hate and a certain loathing
I bear Antonio, that I follow thus
A losing suit against him. Are you answer'd?

Thomas Flatman

An Appeal to Cats in
the Business of Love

Ye cats that at midnight spit at each other,
Who best feel the pangs of a passionate lover,
I appeal to your scratches and your tattered fur,
If the business of Love be no more than to purr.
Old Lady Grimalkin with her gooseberry eyes
Knew something when a kitten, for why she was wise;
You find by experience, the love-fit's soon o'er:
Puss-Puss! lasts not long but turns to *Cat-whore!*
Men ride many miles
Cats tread many tiles
Both hazard their necks in the fray;
Only cats when they fall
From a house or a wall,
Keep their feet, mount their tails, and away!

Lady Jane

Mr. Krook shrunk into his former self as suddenly as he had leaped out of it. 'You see, I have so many things here,' he resumed, holding up the lantern, 'of so many kinds, and all as the neighbours think (but THEY know nothing), wasting away and going to rack and ruin, that that's why they have given me and my place a christening. And I have so many old parchmentses and papers in my stock. And I have a liking for rust and must and cobwebs. And all's fish that comes to my net. And I can't abear to part with anything I once lay hold of (or so my neighbours think, but what do THEY know?) or to alter anything, or to have any sweeping, nor scouring, nor cleaning, nor repairing going on about me. That's the way I've got the ill name of Chancery. I don't mind. I go to see my noble and learned brother pretty well every day, when he sits in the Inn. He don't notice me, but I notice him. There's no great odds betwixt us. We both grub on in a muddle. Hi, Lady Jane!'

A large grey cat leaped from some neighbouring shelf on his shoulder and startled us all.

'Hi! Show 'em how you scratch. Hi! Tear, my lady!' said her master.

The cat leaped down and ripped at a bundle of rags with her tigerish claws, with a sound that it set my teeth on edge to hear.

'She'd do as much for any one I was to set her on,' said the old man. 'I deal in cat-skins among other general matters, and hers was offered to me. It's a very fine skin, as you may see, but I didn't have it stripped off! THAT warn't like Chancery practice though, says you!'

* * *

Mr. Tulkinghorn … comes again to the shop of Mr. Krook, and
enters it straight. It is dim enough, with a blot-headed candle or so
in the windows, and an old man and a cat sitting in the back part
by a fire. The old man rises and comes forward, with another blot-
headed candle in his hand.

'Pray is your lodger within?'

'Male or female, sir?' says Mr. Krook.

'Male. The person who does copying.'

Mr. Krook has eyed his man narrowly. Knows him by sight. Has
an indistinct impression of his aristocratic repute.

'Did you wish to see him, sir?'

'Yes.'

'It's what I seldom do myself,' says Mr. Krook with a grin. 'Shall I
call him down? But it's a weak chance if he'd come, sir!'

'I'll go up to him, then,' says Mr. Tulkinghorn.
'Second floor, sir. Take the candle. Up there!' Mr. Krook, with
his cat beside him, stands at the bottom of the
staircase, looking after Mr. Tulkinghorn.
'Hi-hi!' he says when Mr. Tulkinghorn
has nearly disappeared. The lawyer
looks down over the hand-rail.
The cat expands her wicked
mouth and snarls at him.

'Order, Lady Jane! Behave
yourself to visitors, my lady!'

* * *

Mr. Tulkinghorn with a nod goes
on his way. He comes to the dark
door on the second floor. He knocks,

receives no answer, opens it, and accidentally extinguishes his candle in doing so.

The air of the room is almost bad enough to have extinguished it if he had not. It is a small room, nearly black with soot, and grease, and dirt. In the rusty skeleton of a grate, pinched at the middle as if poverty had gripped it, a red coke fire burns low. In the corner by the chimney stand a deal table and a broken desk, a wilderness marked with a rain of ink. In another corner a ragged old portmanteau on one of the two chairs serves for cabinet or wardrobe; no larger one is needed, for it collapses like the cheeks of a starved man. The floor is bare, except that one old mat, trodden to shreds of rope-yarn, lies perishing upon the hearth. No curtain veils the darkness of the night, but the discoloured shutters are drawn together, and through the two gaunt holes pierced in them, famine might be staring in – the banshee of the man upon the bed.

For, on a low bed opposite the fire, a confusion of dirty patchwork, lean-ribbed ticking, and coarse sacking, the lawyer, hesitating just within the doorway, sees a man. He lies there, dressed in shirt and trousers, with bare feet. He has a yellow look in the spectral darkness of a candle that has guttered down until the whole length of its wick (still burning) has doubled over and left a tower of winding-sheet above it. His hair is ragged, mingling with his whiskers and his beard – the latter, ragged too, and grown, like the scum and mist around him, in neglect. Foul and filthy as the room is, foul and filthy as the air is, it is not easy to perceive what fumes those are which most oppress the senses in it; but through the general sickliness and faintness, and the odour of stale tobacco, there comes into the lawyer's mouth the bitter, vapid taste of opium.

'Hallo, my friend!' he cries, and strikes his iron candlestick against the door.

He thinks he has awakened his friend. He lies a little turned away, but his eyes are surely open.

'Hallo, my friend!' he cries again. 'Hallo! Hallo!'

As he rattles on the door, the candle which has drooped so long goes out and leaves him in the dark, with the gaunt eyes in the shutters staring down upon the bed.

* * *

The welcome light soon shines upon the wall, as Krook comes slowly up with his green-eyed cat following at his heels. 'Does the man generally sleep like this?' inquired the lawyer in a low voice. 'Hi! I don't know,' says Krook, shaking his head and lifting his eyebrows. 'I know next to nothing of his habits except that he keeps himself very close.'

Thus whispering, they both go in together. As the light goes in, the great eyes in the shutters, darkening, seem to close. Not so the eyes upon the bed.

'God save us!' exclaims Mr. Tulkinghorn. 'He is dead!' Krook drops the heavy hand he has taken up so suddenly that the arm swings over the bedside.

They look at one another for a moment.

'Send for some doctor! Call for Miss Flite up the stairs, sir. Here's poison by the bed! Call out for Flite, will you?' says Krook, with his lean hands spread out above the body like a vampire's wings.

Mr. Tulkinghorn hurries to the landing and calls, 'Miss Flite! Flite! Make haste, here, whoever you are! Flite!' Krook follows him with his eyes, and while he is calling, finds opportunity to steal to the old portmanteau and steal back again.

'Run, Flite, run! The nearest doctor! Run!' So Mr. Krook addresses a crazy little woman who is his female lodger, who appears and vanishes in a breath, who soon returns accompanied by a testy medical man brought from his dinner, with a broad, snuffy upper lip and a broad Scotch tongue.

'Ey! Bless the hearts o' ye,' says the medical man, looking up at them after a moment's examination. 'He's just as dead as Phairy!'

* * *

'Don't leave the cat there!' says the surgeon; 'that won't do!' Mr. Krook therefore drives her out before him, and she goes furtively downstairs, winding her lithe tail and licking her lips.

Peter Cristen Asbjörsen, from *East of the Sun and West of the Moon*

The 'Cat' on the *Dovrefell*

Once on a time there was a man up in Finnmark who had caught a great white bear, which he was going to take to the King of Denmark. Now, it so fell out, that he came to the *Dovrefell* just about Christmas Eve, and there he turned into a cottage where a man lived, whose name was Halvor, and asked the man if he could get house-room there for his bear and himself.

'Heaven never help me, if what I say isn't true!' said the man; 'but we can't give anyone house-room just now, for every Christmas Eve such a pack of *Trolls* come down upon us, that we are forced to flit, and haven't so much as a house over our own heads, to say nothing of lending one to anyone else.'

'Oh?' said the man, 'if that's all, you can very well lend me your house; my bear can lie under the stove yonder, and I can sleep in the side-room.'

Well, he begged so hard, that at last he got leave to stay there; so the people of the house flitted out, and before they went, everything was got ready for the *Trolls*; the tables were laid, and there was rice porridge, and fish boiled in lye, and sausages, and all else that was good, just as for any other grand feast.

So, when everything was ready, down came the *Trolls*. Some were great, and some were small; some had long tails, and some had no tails at all; some, too, had long, long noses; and they ate and drank, and tasted everything. Just then one of the little *Trolls* caught sight of the white bear, who lay under the stove; so he took a piece of sausage and stuck it on a fork, and went and poked it up against the bear's nose, screaming out:

'Pussy, will you have some sausage?'

Then the white bear rose up and growled, and hunted the whole pack of them out of doors, both great and small.

Next year Halvor was out in the wood, on the afternoon of Christmas Eve, cutting wood before the holidays, for he thought the *Trolls* would come again; and just as he was hard at work, he heard a voice in the wood calling out:

'Halvor! Halvor!'

'Well,' said Halvor, 'here I am.'

'Have you got your big cat with you still?'

'Yes, that I have,' said Halvor; 'she's lying at home under the stove, and what's more, she has now got seven kittens, far bigger and fiercer than she is herself.'

'Oh, then, we'll never come to see you again,' bawled out the *Troll* away in the wood, and he kept his word; for since that time the *Trolls* have never eaten their Christmas brose with Halvor on the *Dovrefell.*

E. A. Wallis Budge, from *The Book of the Dead*

Feline Goddesses of Ancient Egypt

Sekhmet was in Memphis the wife of Ptah, and the mother of Nefer-Temu and of I-em-hetep. She was the personification of the burning heat of the sun, and as such was the destroyer of the enemies of Ra and Osiris. When Ra determined to punish mankind with death, because they scoffed at him, he sent Sekhmet his 'eye', to perform the work of vengeance … Usually she has the head of a lion surmounted by the sun's disk, round which is a uraeus[3]; and she generally holds a sceptre, but sometimes a knife.

Bast, according to one legend, was the mother of Nefer-Temu. She was the personification of the gentle and fructifying heat of the sun, as opposed to that personified by Sekhmet. The cat was sacred to Bast, and the goddess is usually depicted cat-headed. The most famous seat of her worship was the city of Bubastis.

---

3 A protective rearing cobra.

Ancient Egyptian Cats

[66] Domestic animals are numerous – and would be even more so, were it not for something that serves to keep the cat population down. Female cats which have given birth to kittens will have nothing more to do with males; the male cats are thereby left as frustrated as they are needy. This has driven them to devise a cunning plan: they snatch or steal the kittens from their mother, and then dispose of them. (But though they kill the kittens, they do not eat them.) The females, bereft of their offspring, and eager for more, due to their love for babies, then return to the males. In the event of a fire, what happens to cats is uncanny in the extreme. The Egyptians, rather than attempting to extinguish the flames, instead form a human chain and keep watch over the cats; the cats, however, slipping through the line of men, or else jumping over it, hurl themselves into the conflagration. An event such as this causes the Egyptians great distress. All the inhabitants of a household in which a cat has died of natural causes will shave off their eyebrows, and nothing else; but if a dog dies, then the entire body and head are shaved.

[67] Following their death, cats are borne away to the city of Bubastis, where they are mummified and buried in sacral pits.

Jaromir Malek

from *The Cat in Ancient Egypt*

The modern Egyptian domestic cat, which one encounters in the cafes and bazaars, in the noisy streets of Cairo and in the dusty sun-drenched villages, is a graceful and delicate little creature, usually much smaller than Western cats. The intensity of its attentive gaze is unnerving and almost tangible; the speed of its lightning reactions makes you gasp. It is hard to believe that the ancestors of this entertaining but humble animal played such an important part in everyday life in ancient Egypt.

Where did it all begin? One of the closest wild relatives of the modern cat was *Felix silvestris libyca*, or the African wild cat, with tawny, yellow-grey fur and striped markings which provided ideal camouflage among the rocks and sand of the desert. This was a larger beast than the little cats of today: a predator rather than a scavenger. Occasionally, among the multi-coloured cats of modern Egypt, one can still see an animal that seems to revert to its ancient ancestry. Several years ago I saw such a one climbing the Great Pyramid of King Khufu (2549–2526 BC) at Giza – an animal with superb yellow and cream fur, brindled with fine lines of silvery grey. It is strictly forbidden to climb the pyramids, but this prohibition cannot, of course, be enforced on cats, and the cat was making its way upwards, safe from all human interference, its coat blending perfectly with the rugged texture of the ancient stones. No doubt, there would be plenty of prey on the pyramid, in the shape of careless birds, and perhaps small creatures such as lizards. In the suffocating heat and the blinding sun the cat calmly went about its own private concerns, high above the mass of humanity milling about below and with total disregard for their incomprehensible trivial pursuits.

The Cat that Walked by Himself

Hear and attend and listen; for this befell and behappened and became and was, O my Best Beloved, when the Tame animals were wild. The Dog was wild, and the Horse was wild, and the Cow was wild, and the Sheep was wild, and the Pig was wild – as wild as wild could be – and they walked in the Wet Wild Woods by their wild lones. But the wildest of all the wild animals was the Cat. He walked by himself, and all places were alike to him.

Of course the Man was wild too. He was dreadfully wild. He didn't even begin to be tame till he met the Woman, and she told him that she did not like living in his wild ways. She picked out a nice dry Cave, instead of a heap of wet leaves, to lie down in; and she strewed clean sand on the floor; and she lit a nice fire of wood at the back of the Cave; and she hung a dried wild-horse skin, tail-down, across the opening of the Cave; and she said, 'Wipe your feet, dear, when you come in, and now we'll keep house.'

That night, Best Beloved, they ate wild sheep roasted on the hot stones, and flavoured with wild garlic and wild pepper; and wild duck stuffed with wild rice and wild fenugreek and wild coriander; and marrowbones of wild oxen; and wild cherries, and wild grenadillas. Then the Man went to sleep in front of the fire ever so happy; but the Woman sat up, combing her hair. She took the bone of the shoulder of mutton – the big fat blade-bone – and she looked at the wonderful marks on it, and she threw more wood on the fire, and she made a Magic. She made the First Singing Magic in the world.

Out in the Wet Wild Woods all the wild animals gathered together where they could see the light of the fire a long way off, and they wondered what it meant.

Then Wild Horse stamped with his wild foot and said, 'O my
Friends and O my Enemies, why have the Man and the Woman
made that great light in that great Cave, and what harm will it do us?'

Wild Dog lifted up his wild nose and smelled the smell of roast
mutton, and said, 'I will go up and see and look, and say; for I think
it is good. Cat, come with me.'

'Nenni!' said the Cat. 'I am the Cat who walks by himself, and all
places are alike to me. I will not come.'

'Then we can never be friends again,' said Wild Dog, and he
trotted off to the Cave. But when he had gone a little way the Cat
said to himself, 'All places are alike to me. Why should I not go too
and see and look and come away at my own liking?' So he slipped
after Wild Dog softly, very softly, and hid himself where he could
hear everything.

When Wild Dog reached the mouth of the Cave he lifted up the
dried horse-skin with his nose and sniffed the beautiful smell of the
roast mutton, and the Woman, looking at the blade-bone, heard
him, and laughed, and said, 'Here comes the first. Wild Thing out
of the Wild Woods, what do you want?'

Wild Dog said, 'O my Enemy and Wife of my Enemy, what is
this that smells so good in the Wild Woods?'

Then the Woman picked up a roasted mutton-bone and threw it
to Wild Dog, and said, 'Wild Thing out of the Wild Woods, taste
and try.' Wild Dog gnawed the bone, and it was more delicious
than anything he had ever tasted, and he said, 'O my Enemy and
Wife of my Enemy, give me another.'

The Woman said, 'Wild Thing out of the Wild Woods, help my
Man to hunt through the day and guard this Cave at night, and I
will give you as many roast bones as you need.'

'Ah!' said the Cat, listening. 'This is a very wise Woman, but she
is not so wise as I am.'

Wild Dog crawled into the Cave and laid his head on the Woman's lap, and said, 'O my Friend and Wife of my Friend, I will help Your Man to hunt through the day, and at night I will guard your Cave.'

'Ah!' said the Cat, listening. 'That is a very foolish Dog.' And he went back through the Wet Wild Woods waving his wild tail, and walking by his wild lone. But he never told anybody.

When the Man waked up he said, 'What is Wild Dog doing here?' And the Woman said, 'His name is not Wild Dog any more, but the First Friend, because he will be our friend for always and always and always. Take him with you when you go hunting.'

Next night the Woman cut great green armfuls of fresh grass from the water-meadows, and dried it before the fire, so that it smelt like new-mown hay, and she sat at the mouth of the Cave and plaited a halter out of horse-hide, and she looked at the shoulder-of-mutton-bone – at the big broad blade-bone – and she made a Magic. She made the Second Singing Magic in the world.

Out in the Wild Woods all the wild animals wondered what had happened to Wild Dog, and at last Wild Horse stamped with his foot and said, 'I will go and see and say why Wild Dog has not returned. Cat, come with me.'

'Nenni!' said the Cat. 'I am the Cat who walks by himself, and all places are alike to me. I will not come.' But all the same he followed Wild Horse softly, very softly, and hid himself where he could hear everything.

When the Woman heard Wild Horse tripping and stumbling on his long mane, she laughed and said, 'Here comes the second. Wild Thing out of the Wild Woods, what do you want?'

Wild Horse said, 'O my Enemy and Wife of my Enemy, where is Wild Dog?'

The Woman laughed, and picked up the blade-bone and looked at it, and said, 'Wild Thing out of the Wild Woods, you did not come here for Wild Dog, but for the sake of this good grass.'

And Wild Horse, tripping and stumbling on his long mane, said, 'That is true; give it me to eat.'

The Woman said, 'Wild Thing out of the Wild Woods, bend your wild head and wear what I give you, and you shall eat the wonderful grass three times a day.'

'Ah,' said the Cat, listening, 'this is a clever Woman, but she is not so clever as I am.'

Wild Horse bent his wild head, and the Woman slipped the plaited hide halter over it, and Wild Horse breathed on the Woman's feet and said, 'O my Mistress, and Wife of my Master, I will be your servant for the sake of the wonderful grass.'

'Ah,' said the Cat, listening, 'that is a very foolish Horse.' And he went back through the Wet Wild Woods, waving his wild tail and walking by his wild lone. But he never told anybody.

When the Man and the Dog came back from hunting, the Man said, 'What is Wild Horse doing here?' And the Woman said, 'His name is not Wild Horse any more, but the First Servant, because he will carry us from place to place for always and always and always. Ride on his back when you go hunting.'

Next day, holding her wild head high that her wild horns should not catch in the wild trees, Wild Cow came up to the Cave, and the Cat followed, and hid himself just the same as before; and everything happened just the same as before; and the Cat said the same things as before, and when Wild Cow had promised to give her milk to the Woman every day in exchange for the wonderful grass, the Cat went back through the Wet Wild Woods waving his wild tail and walking by his wild lone, just the same as before. But he never told anybody. And when the Man and the Horse and the Dog came home from hunting and asked the same questions same as before, the Woman said, 'Her name is not Wild Cow any more,

but the Giver of Good Food. She will give us the warm white milk
for always and always and always, and I will take care of her while
you and the First Friend and the First Servant go hunting.'

Next day the Cat waited to see if any other Wild thing would go
up to the Cave, but no one moved in the Wet Wild Woods, so the
Cat walked there by himself; and he saw the Woman milking the
Cow, and he saw the light of the fire in the Cave, and he smelt the
smell of the warm white milk.

Cat said, 'O my Enemy and Wife of my Enemy, where did Wild
Cow go?'

The Woman laughed and said, 'Wild Thing out of the Wild
Woods, go back to the Woods again, for I have braided up my hair,
and I have put away the magic blade-bone, and we have no more
need of either friends or servants in our Cave.'

Cat said, 'I am not a friend, and I am not a servant. I am the Cat
who walks by himself, and I wish to come into your cave.'

Woman said, 'Then why did you not come with First Friend on
the first night?'

Cat grew very angry and said, 'Has Wild Dog told tales of me?'

Then the Woman laughed and said, 'You are the Cat who walks
by himself, and all places are alike to you. You are neither a friend
nor a servant. You have said it yourself. Go away and walk by
yourself in all places alike.'

Then Cat pretended to be sorry and said, 'Must I never come
into the Cave? Must I never sit by the warm fire? Must I never drink
the warm white milk? You are very wise and very beautiful. You
should not be cruel even to a Cat.'

Woman said, 'I knew I was wise, but I did not know I was
beautiful. So I will make a bargain with you. If ever I say one word
in your praise you may come into the Cave.'

'And if you say two words in my praise?' said the Cat.

'I never shall,' said the Woman, 'but if I say two words in your praise, you may sit by the fire in the Cave.'

'And if you say three words?' said the Cat.

'I never shall,' said the Woman, 'but if I say three words in your praise, you may drink the warm white milk three times a day for always and always and always.'

Then the Cat arched his back and said, 'Now let the Curtain at the mouth of the Cave, and the Fire at the back of the Cave, and the Milk-pots that stand beside the Fire, remember what my Enemy and the Wife of my Enemy has said.' And he went away through the Wet Wild Woods waving his wild tail and walking by his wild lone.

That night when the Man and the Horse and the Dog came home from hunting, the Woman did not tell them of the bargain that she had made with the Cat, because she was afraid that they might not like it.

Cat went far and far away and hid himself in the Wet Wild Woods by his wild lone for a long time till the Woman forgot all about him. Only the Bat – the little upside-down Bat – that hung inside the Cave, knew where Cat hid; and every evening Bat would fly to Cat with news of what was happening.

One evening Bat said, 'There is a Baby in the Cave. He is new and pink and fat and small, and the Woman is very fond of him.'

'Ah,' said the Cat, listening, 'but what is the Baby fond of?'

'He is fond of things that are soft and tickle,' said the Bat. 'He is fond of warm things to hold in his arms when he goes to sleep. He is fond of being played with. He is fond of all those things.'

'Ah,' said the Cat, listening, 'then my time has come.'

Next night Cat walked through the Wet Wild Woods and hid very near the Cave till morning-time, and Man and Dog and Horse went hunting. The Woman was busy cooking that morning, and

the Baby cried and interrupted. So she carried him outside the
Cave and gave him a handful of pebbles to play with. But still the
Baby cried.

Then the Cat put out his paddy paw and patted the Baby on the
cheek, and it cooed; and the Cat rubbed against its fat knees and
tickled it under its fat chin with his tail. And the Baby laughed; and
the Woman heard him and smiled.

Then the Bat – the little upside-down bat – that hung in the
mouth of the Cave said, 'O my Hostess and Wife of my Host and
Mother of my Host's Son, a Wild Thing from the Wild Woods is
most beautifully playing with your Baby.'

'A blessing on that Wild Thing whoever he may be,' said the
Woman, straightening her back, 'for I was a busy woman this
morning and he has done me a service.'

That very minute and second, Best Beloved, the dried horse-skin
Curtain that was stretched tail-down at the mouth of the Cave fell
down – *woosh!* – because it remembered the bargain she had made
with the Cat, and when the Woman went to pick it up – lo and
behold! – the Cat was sitting quite comfy inside the Cave.

'O my Enemy and Wife of my Enemy and Mother of my Enemy,'
said the Cat, 'it is I: for you have spoken a word in my praise, and
now I can sit within the Cave for always and always and always.
But still I am the Cat who walks by himself, and all places are alike
to me.'

The Woman was very angry, and shut her lips tight and took up
her spinning-wheel and began to spin.

But the Baby cried because the Cat had gone away, and the
Woman could not hush it, for it struggled and kicked and grew
black in the face.

'O my Enemy and Wife of my Enemy and Mother of my Enemy,'
said the Cat, 'take a strand of the wire that you are spinning and

tie it to your spinning-whorl and drag it along the floor, and I will
show you a Magic that shall make your Baby laugh as loudly as he
is now crying.'

'I will do so,' said the Woman, 'because I am at my wits' end; but
I will not thank you for it.'

She tied the thread to the little clay spindle-whorl and drew
it across the floor, and the Cat ran after it and patted it with his
paws and rolled head over heels, and tossed it backward over his
shoulder and chased it between his hind-legs and pretended to lose
it, and pounced down upon it again, till the Baby laughed as loudly
as it had been crying, and scrambled after the Cat and frolicked all
over the Cave till it grew tired and settled down to sleep with the
Cat in its arms.

'Now,' said the Cat, 'I will sing the Baby a song that shall keep
him asleep for an hour.' And he began to purr, loud and low, low
and loud, till the Baby fell fast asleep. The Woman smiled as she
looked down upon the two of them and said, 'That was wonderfully
done. No question but you are very clever, O Cat.'

That very minute and second, Best Beloved, the smoke of the fire
at the back of the Cave came down in clouds from the roof – *puff!* –
because it remembered the bargain she had made with the Cat, and
when it had cleared away – lo and behold! – the Cat was sitting
quite comfy close to the fire.

'O my Enemy and Wife of my Enemy and Mother of My Enemy,'
said the Cat, 'it is I, for you have spoken a second word in my
praise, and now I can sit by the warm fire at the back of the Cave
for always and always and always. But still I am the Cat who walks
by himself, and all places are alike to me.'

Then the Woman was very very angry, and let down her hair and
put more wood on the fire and brought out the broad blade-bone
of the shoulder of mutton and began to make a Magic that should

prevent her from saying a third word in praise of the Cat. It was
not a Singing Magic, Best Beloved, it was a Still Magic; and by and
by the Cave grew so still that a little wee-wee mouse crept out of a
corner and ran across the floor.

'O my Enemy and Wife of my Enemy and Mother of my Enemy,'
said the Cat, 'is that little mouse part of your magic?'

'Ouh! Chee! No indeed!' said the Woman, and she dropped the
blade-bone and jumped upon the footstool in front of the fire and
braided up her hair very quick for fear that the mouse should run
up it.

'Ah,' said the Cat, watching, 'then the mouse will do me no harm
if I eat it?'

'No,' said the Woman, braiding up her hair, 'eat it quickly and I
will ever be grateful to you.'

Cat made one jump and caught the little mouse, and the Woman
said, 'A hundred thanks. Even the First Friend is not quick enough
to catch little mice as you have done. You must be very wise.'

That very moment and second, O Best Beloved, the Milk-pot that
stood by the fire cracked in two pieces – * fffft!* – because it remembered
the bargain she had made with the Cat; and when the Woman
jumped down from the footstool – lo and behold! – the Cat was
lapping up the warm white milk that lay in one of the broken pieces.

'O my Enemy and Wife of my Enemy and Mother of my Enemy,
said the Cat, 'it is I: for you have spoken three words in my praise,
and now I can drink the warm white milk three times a day for
always and always and always. But still I am the Cat who walks by
himself, and all places are alike to me.'

Then the Woman laughed and set the Cat a bowl of the warm
white milk and said, 'O Cat, you are as clever as a man, but
remember that your bargain was not made with the Man or the
Dog, and I do not know what they will do when they come home.'

'What is that to me?' said the Cat. 'If I have my place in the Cave by the fire and my warm white milk three times a day I do not care what the Man or the Dog can do.'

That evening when the Man and the Dog came into the Cave, the Woman told them all the story of the bargain while the Cat sat by the fire and smiled. Then the Man said, 'Yes, but he has not made a bargain with *me* or with all proper Men after me.' Then he took off his two leather boots and he took up his little stone axe (that makes three) and he fetched a piece of wood and a hatchet (that is five altogether), and he set them out in a row and he said, 'Now we will make our bargain. If you do not catch mice when you are in the Cave for always and always and always, I will throw these five things at you whenever I see you, and so shall all proper Men do after me.'

'Ah,' said the Woman, listening, 'this is a very clever Cat, but he is not so clever as my Man.'

The Cat counted the five things (and they looked very knobby) and he said, 'I will catch mice when I am in the Cave for always and always and always; but *still* I am the Cat who walks by himself, and all places are alike to me.'

'Not when I am near,' said the Man. 'If you had not said that last I would have put all these things away for always and always and always; but I am now going to throw my two boots and my little stone axe (that makes three) at you whenever I meet you. And so shall all proper Men do after me!'

Then the Dog said, 'Wait a minute. He has not made a bargain with me or with all proper Dogs after me.' And he showed his teeth and said, 'If you are not kind to the Baby while I am in the Cave for always and always and always, I will hunt you till I catch you, and when I catch you I will bite you. And so shall all proper Dogs do after me.'

'Ah,' said the Woman, listening, 'this is a very clever Cat, but he is not so clever as the Dog.'

Cat counted the Dog's teeth (and they looked very pointed) and he said, 'I will be kind to the Baby while I am in the Cave, as long as he does not pull my tail too hard, for always and always and always. But still I am the Cat that walks by himself, and all places are alike to me!'

'Not when I am near,' said the Dog. 'If you had not said that last I would have shut my mouth for always and always and always; but *now* I am going to hunt you up a tree whenever I meet you. And so shall all proper Dogs do after me.'

Then the Man threw his two boots and his little stone axe (that makes three) at the Cat, and the Cat ran out of the Cave and the Dog chased him up a tree; and from that day to this, Best Beloved, three proper Men out of five will always throw things at a Cat whenever they meet him, and all proper Dogs will chase him up a tree. But the Cat keeps his side of the bargain too. He will kill mice and he will be kind to Babies when he is in the house, just as long as they do not pull his tail too hard. But when he has done that, and between times, and when the moon gets up and night comes, he is the Cat that walks by himself, and all places are alike to him. Then he goes out to the Wet Wild Woods or up the Wet Wild Trees or on the Wet Wild Roofs, waving his wild tail and walking by his wild lone.

Traditional

Nursery Rhymes

Hey diddle diddle,
The Cat and the fiddle,
The Cow jumped over the moon.
The little Dog laughed,
To see such sport,
And the Dish ran away with the Spoon.

* * *

There was a crooked man, and he walked a crooked mile,
He found a crooked sixpence against a crooked stile:
He bought a crooked cat, which caught a crooked mouse,
And they all lived together in a little crooked house.

* * *

Pussy cat, pussy cat
Where have you been?
I've been to London
To look at the Queen

Pussy cat, pussy cat
What did you there?
I frightened a little Mouse
Under her chair.

* * *

Ding dong bell,
Pussy's in the well!
Who put her in?
Little Johnny Green.
Who pulled her out?
Big Johnny Stout.
What a naughty boy was that
To try to drown poor pussy cat,
Who never did him any harm,
But killed the mice in his father's barn!

Edward Lear

The Owl and the Pussycat

The Owl and the Pussycat went to sea
In a beautiful pea-green boat,
They took some honey, and plenty of money.
Wrapped up in a five-pound note.
The Owl looked up to the stars above,
And sang to a small guitar,
'O lovely Pussy! O Pussy, my love,
What a beautiful Pussy you are,
You are
You are!
What a beautiful Pussy you are!'

Pussy said to the Owl, 'You elegant fowl!
How charmingly sweet you sing!
O let us be married! too long we have tarried:
But what shall we do for a ring?'
They sailed away for a year and a day,
To the land where the Bong-tree grows
And there in a wood a Piggy-wig stood
With a ring at the end of his nose,
His nose,
His nose,
With a ring at the end of his nose.

'Dear Pig, are you willing to sell for one shilling
Your ring?' Said the Piggy, 'I will.'
So they took it away, and were married next day

By the Turkey who lives on the hill.
They dined on mince, and slices of quince,
Which they ate with a runcible spoon;
And hand in hand, on the edge of the sand,
They danced by the light of the moon,
The moon,
The moon,
They danced by the light of the moon.

Gulliver Encounters the Giants' Cat

A servant brought in dinner … The company were the farmer and his wife, three children and an old grandmother: when they were sat down, the farmer placed me at some distance from him on the table, which was thirty foot high from the floor. I was in a terrible fright, and kept as far as I could from the edge for fear of falling. The wife minced a bit of meat, then crumbled some bread on a trencher, and placed it before me.

* * *

In the midst of dinner my mistress's favourite cat leapt into her lap. I heard a noise behind me like that of a dozen stocking-weavers at work; and turning my head I found it proceeded from the purring of this animal, who seemed to be three times larger than an ox, as I computed by the view of her head, and one of her paws, while her mistress was feeding and stroking her. The fierceness of this creature's countenance altogether discomposed me; though I stood at the farther end of the table, above fifty foot off, and although my mistress held her fast for fear she might give a spring, and seize me in her talons. But it happened there was no danger; for the cat took not the least notice of me when my master placed me within three yards of her. And as I have always been told, and found true by experience in my travels, that flying, or discovering fear before a fierce animal, is a certain way to make it pursue or attack you, so I resolved in this dangerous juncture to show no manner of concern. I walked with intrepidity five or six times before the very head of the cat, and came within half a yard of her; whereupon she drew herself back, as if she were more afraid of me.

La Fontaine and de la Rochefoucault

Rochefoucault. Pray do not move on any account; above all, lest you should disturb that amiable grey cat, fast asleep in his innocence on your shoulder.

La Fontaine. Ah, rogue! art thou there? Why! thou hast not licked my face this half-hour.

Rochefoucault. And more, too, I should imagine. I do not judge from his somnolency, which, if he were President of the Parliament, could not be graver, but from his natural sagacity. Cats weigh practicabilities. What sort of tongue has he?

La Fontaine. He has the roughest tongue and the tenderest heart of any cat in Paris. If you observe the colour of his coat, it is rather blue than grey; a certain indication of goodness in these contemplative creatures.

Rochefoucault. We were talking of his tongue alone; by which cats, like men, are flatterers.

La Fontaine. Ah! you gentlemen of the court are much mistaken in thinking that vices have so extensive a range. There are some of our vices, like some of our diseases, from which the quadrupeds are exempt; and those, both diseases and vices, are the most discreditable.

Rochefoucault. I do not bear patiently any evil spoken of the court: for it must be acknowledged, by the most malicious, that the court is the purifier of the whole nation.

La Fontaine. I know little of the court, and less of the whole nation; but how can this be?

Rochefoucault. It collects all ramblers and gamblers; all the market-men and market-women who deal in articles which God has thrown into their baskets, without any trouble on their part; all the seducers and all who wish to be seduced; all the duellists who erase their crimes with their swords, and sweat out their cowardice with daily practice; all the nobles whose patents of nobility lie in gold snuff-boxes, or have worn Mechlin ruffles, or are deposited within the archives of knee-deep waistcoats; all stock-jobbers and church-jobbers, the black-legged and the red-legged game, the flower of the *justaucorps,* the *robe,* and the *soutane.* If these were spread over the surface of France, instead of close compressure in the court or cabinet, they would corrupt the whole country in two years. As matters now stand, it will require a quarter of a century to effect it.

La Fontaine. Am I not right then in preferring my beasts to yours? But if yours were loose, mine (as you prove to me,) would be the last to suffer by it, poor dear creatures! Speaking of cats, I would have avoided all personality that might be offensive to them: I would not exactly have said, in so many words, that, by their tongues, they are flatterers, like men. Language may take a turn advantageously in favour of our friends. True, we resemble all animals in something. I am quite ashamed and mortified that your lordship, or anybody, should have had the start of me in this reflection. When a cat flatters with his tongue he is not insincere:

you may safely take it for a real kindness. He is loyal, M. de la Rochefoucault! my word for him, he is loyal. Observe too, if you please, no cat ever licks you when he wants anything from you; so that there is nothing of baseness in such an act of adulation, if we must call it so. For my part, I am slow to designate by so foul a name, that (be it what it may) which is subsequent to a kindness. Cats ask plainly for what they want.

Rochefoucault. And, if they can not get it by protocols they get it by invasion and assault.

La Fontaine. No! no! usually they go elsewhere, and fondle those from whom they obtain it. In this I see no resemblance to invaders and conquerors. I draw no parallels: I would excite no heart-burnings between us and them. Let all have their due.

I do not like to lift this creature off, for it would waken him, else I could find out, by some subsequent action, the reason why he has not been on the alert to lick my cheek for so long a time.

Rochefoucault. Cats are wary and provident. He would not enter into any contest with you, however friendly.

Mervyn Peake, from *Titus Groan*

The Cat Room

'Cat room,' said Flay, putting his hand to the iron knob of the door.

'Oh,' said Steerpike, thinking hard, and repeating 'Cat room' to fill in time, for he saw no reason for the remark. The only interpretation he could give to the ejaculation was that Flay was referring to him as a cat and asking to be given more room. Yet there had been no irritation in the voice.

A room was filled with the late sunbeams. Steerpike stood quite still, a twinge of pleasure running through his body. He grinned. A carpet filled the floor with blue pasture. Thereon were seated in a hundred decorative attitudes, or stood immobile like carvings, or walked superbly across their sapphire setting, inter-weaving with each other like a living arabesque, a swarm of snow-white cats.

As Mr Flay passed down the centre of the room, Steerpike could not but notice the contrast between the dark rambling figure with his ungainly movements and the monotonous cracking of his knees, the contrast between this and the superb elegance and silence of the white cats. They took not the slightest notice of either Mr Flay or of himself save for the sudden cessation of their purring. When they had stood in the darkness, and before Mr Flay had removed the bunch of keys from his pocket, Steerpike had imagined he had heard a heavy, deep throbbing, a monotonous sea-like drumming of sound, and he now knew that it must have been the pullulation of the cats.

As they passed through a carved archway at the far end of the room and had closed the door behind them he heard the vibration of their throats, for now that the white cats were once more alone it was revived, and the deep unhurried purring was like the voice of an ocean in the throat of a shell.

Traditional, from *Fairy and Folk Tales of the Irish Peasantry*
edited by William Butler Yeats

The Demon Cat

There was a woman in Connemara, the wife of a fisherman; as he
had always good luck, she had plenty of fish at all times stored
away in the house ready for market. But, to her great annoyance,
she found that a great cat used to come in at night and devour
all the best and finest fish. So she kept a big stick by her, and
determined to watch.

One day, as she and a woman were spinning together, the house
suddenly became quite dark; and the door was burst open as if by
the blast of the tempest, when in walked a huge black cat, who went
straight up to the fire, then turned round and growled at them.

'Why, surely this is the devil,' said a young girl, who was by,
sorting fish.

'I'll teach you how to call me names,' said the cat; and, jumping
at her, he scratched her arm till the blood came. 'There, now,' he
said, 'you will be more civil another time when a gentleman comes
to see you.' And with that he walked over to the door and shut it
close, to prevent any of them going out, for the poor young girl,
while crying loudly from fright and pain, had made a desperate
rush to get away.

Just then a man was going by, and hearing the cries, he pushed
open the door and tried to get in; but the cat stood on the
threshold, and would let no one pass. On this the man attacked
him with his stick, and gave him a sound blow; the cat, however,
was more than a match in the fight, for it flew at him and tore his
face and hands so badly that the man at last took to his heels and
ran away as fast as he could.

'Now, it's time for my dinner,' said the cat, going up to examine
the fish that was laid out on the tables. 'I hope the fish is good
to-day. Now, don't disturb me, nor make a fuss; I can help myself.'
With that he jumped up, and began to devour all the best fish,
while he growled at the woman.

'Away, out of this, you wicked beast,' she cried, giving it a blow
with the tongs that would have broken its back, only it was a devil;
'out of this; no fish shall you have to-day.'

But the cat only grinned at her, and went on tearing and spoiling
and devouring the fish, evidently not a bit the worse for the blow.
On this, both the women attacked it with sticks, and struck hard
blows enough to kill it, on which the cat glared at them, and spit
fire; then, making a leap, it tore their heads and arms till the blood
came, and the frightened women rushed shrieking from the house.

But presently the mistress returned, carrying with her a bottle
of holy water; and, looking in, she saw the cat still devouring the
fish, and not minding. So she crept over quietly and threw holy
water on it without a word. No sooner was this done than a dense
black smoke filled the place, through which nothing was seen but
the two red eyes of the cat, burning like coals of fire. Then the
smoke gradually cleared away, and she saw the body of the creature
burning slowly till it became shrivelled and black like a cinder,
and finally disappeared. And from that time the fish remained
untouched and safe from harm, for the power of the evil one was
broken, and the demon cat was seen no more.

John Gribbin

from *In Search of Schrödinger's Cat*

The concept behind this thought experiment is very simple.
Schrödinger suggested that we should imagine a box that contains
a radioactive source, a detector that records the presence of
radioactive particles (a Geiger counter, perhaps) and a glass bottle
containing a poison such as cyanide, and a live cat. The apparatus
in the box is arranged so that the detector is switched on for just
long enough so that there is a fifty-fifty chance that one of the
atoms in the radioactive material will decay and that the detector
will record a particle. If the detector does record such an event,
then the glass container is crushed and the cat dies; if not, the cat
lives. We have no way of knowing the outcome of this experiment
until we open the box to look inside; radioactive decay occurs
entirely by chance and is unpredictable except in a statistical sense.
According to the strict Copenhagen interpretation … the equal
probabilities for radioactive decay and no radioactive decay should
produce a superposition of states. The whole experiment, cat and
all, is governed by the rule that the superposition is 'real' until we
look at the experiment, and that only at the instant of observation
does the wave function collapse into one of the two states. Until
we look inside, there is a radioactive sample that has both decayed
and not decayed, a glass vessel of poison that is neither broken nor
unbroken, and a cat that is both dead and alive, neither alive nor
dead. Quantum theory really is this weird.

It is one thing to imagine an elementary particle such as an
electron being neither here nor there but in some superposition
of states, but much harder to imagine a familiar thing like a cat
in this form of suspended animation. Schrödinger thought up the

example to establish that there is a flaw in the strict Copenhagen interpretation, since obviously the cat cannot be both alive and dead at the same time. But is this any more 'obvious' than the fact that an electron cannot be both a wave and a particle at the same time? Common sense has already been tested as a guide to quantum reality and been found wanting. The one sure thing we know about the quantum world is not to trust our common sense and only to believe things we can see directly or detect unambiguously with our instruments. We don't know what goes on inside a box unless we look.

Arguments about the cat in the box have gone on ever since. One school of thought says there is no problem, because the cat is quite able to decide for itself whether it is alive or dead, and the cat's consciousness is sufficient to trigger the collapse of the wave function.

Edgar Allan Poe

The Black Cat

For the most wild, yet most homely narrative which I am about to pen, I neither expect nor solicit belief. Mad indeed would I be to expect it, in a case where my very senses reject their own evidence. Yet, mad am I not – and very surely do I not dream. But to-morrow I die, and to-day I would unburden my soul. My immediate purpose is to place before the world, plainly, succinctly, and without comment, a series of mere household events. In their consequences, these events have terrified – have tortured – have destroyed me. Yet I will not attempt to expound them. To me, they have presented little but Horror – to many they will seem less terrible than *baroques*. Hereafter, perhaps, some intellect may be found which will reduce my phantasm to the commonplace – some intellect more calm, more logical, and far less excitable than my own, which will perceive, in the circumstances I detail with awe, nothing more than an ordinary succession of very natural causes and effects.

From my infancy I was noted for the docility and humanity of my disposition. My tenderness of heart was even so conspicuous as to make me the jest of my companions. I was especially fond of animals, and was indulged by my parents with a great variety of pets. With these I spent most of my time, and never was so happy as when feeding and caressing them. This peculiarity of character grew with my growth, and in my manhood, I derived from it one of my principal sources of pleasure. To those who have cherished an affection for a faithful and sagacious dog, I need hardly be at the trouble of explaining the nature or the intensity of the gratification thus derivable. There is something in the unselfish and self-sacrificing love of a brute, which goes directly to the heart of him who has had frequent occasion to test the paltry friendship and gossamer fidelity of mere *Man*.

I married early, and was happy to find in my wife a disposition not uncongenial with my own. Observing my partiality for domestic pets, she lost no opportunity of procuring those of the most agreeable kind. We had birds, gold-fish, a fine dog, rabbits, a small monkey and a *cat*.

This latter was a remarkably large and beautiful animal, entirely black, and sagacious to an astonishing degree. In speaking of his intelligence, my wife, who at heart was not a little tinctured with superstition, made frequent allusion to the ancient popular notion, which regarded all black cats as witches in disguise. Not that she was ever *serious* upon this point – and I mention the matter at all for no better reason than that it happens, just now, to be remembered.

Pluto – this was the cat's name – was my favorite pet and playmate. I alone fed him, and he attended me wherever I went about the house. It was even with difficulty that I could prevent him from following me through the streets.

Our friendship lasted, in this manner, for several years, during which my general temperament and character – through the instrumentality of the Fiend Intemperance – had (I blush to confess it) experienced a radical alteration for the worse. I grew, day by day, more moody, more irritable, more regardless of the feelings of others. I suffered myself to use intemperate language to my wife. At length, I even offered her personal violence. My pets, of course, were made to feel the change in my disposition. I not only neglected, but ill-used them. For Pluto, however, I still retained sufficient regard to restrain me from maltreating him, as I made no scruple of maltreating the rabbits, the monkey, or even the dog, when by accident, or through affection, they came in my way. But my disease grew upon me – for what disease is like Alcohol! – and at length even Pluto, who was now becoming old, and consequently somewhat peevish – even Pluto began to experience the effects of my ill temper.

One night, returning home, much intoxicated, from one of my haunts about town, I fancied that the cat avoided my presence. I seized him; when, in his fright at my violence, he inflicted a slight wound upon my hand with his teeth. The fury of a demon instantly possessed me. I knew myself no longer. My original soul seemed, at once, to take its flight from my body; and a more than fiendish malevolence, gin-nurtured, thrilled every fibre of my frame. I took from my waistcoat-pocket a penknife, opened it, grasped the poor beast by the throat and deliberately cut one of its eyes from the socket! I blush, I burn, I shudder, while I pen the damnable atrocity.

When reason returned with the morning – when I had slept off the fumes of the night's debauch – I experienced a sentiment half of horror, half of remorse, for the crime of which I had been guilty; but it was, at best, a feeble and equivocal feeling, and the soul remained untouched. I again plunged into excess, and soon drowned in wine all memory of the deed.

In the meantime the cat slowly recovered. The socket of the lost eye presented, it is true, a frightful appearance, but he no longer appeared to suffer any pain. He went about the house as usual, but, as might be expected, fled in extreme terror at my approach. I had so much of my old heart left, as to be at first grieved by this evident dislike on the part of a creature which had once so loved me. But this feeling soon gave place to irritation. And then came, as if to my final and irrevocable overthrow, the spirit of PERVERSENESS. Of this spirit philosophy takes no account. Yet I am not more sure that my soul lives, than I am that perverseness is one of the primitive impulses of the human heart – one of the indivisible primary faculties, or sentiments, which give direction to the character of Man. Who has not, a hundred times, found himself committing a vile or a stupid action, for no other reason than because he knows he should *not*? Have we not a perpetual inclination, in the teeth of our best judgment, to violate that which is *Law*, merely because we understand it to be such? This spirit of perverseness, I say, came to my final overthrow. It was this unfathomable longing of the soul *to vex itself* – to offer violence to its own nature – to do wrong for the wrong's sake only – that urged me to continue and finally to consummate the injury I had inflicted upon the unoffending brute. One morning, in cold blood, I slipped a noose about its neck and hung it to the limb of a tree; – hung it with the tears streaming from my eyes, and with the bitterest remorse at my heart; – hung it *because* I knew that it had loved me, and *because* I felt it had given me no reason of offence; – hung it *because* I knew that in so doing I was committing a sin – a deadly sin that would so jeopardize my immortal soul as to place it – if such a thing wore possible – even beyond the reach of the infinite mercy of the Most Merciful and Most Terrible God.

On the night of the day on which this cruel deed was done, I was aroused from sleep by the cry of fire. The curtains of my bed were in flames. The whole house was blazing. It was with great difficulty that my wife, a servant and myself, made our escape from the conflagration. The destruction was complete. My entire worldly wealth was swallowed up, and I resigned myself thenceforward to despair.

I am above the weakness of seeking to establish a sequence of cause and effect, between the disaster and the atrocity. But I am detailing a chain of facts – and wish not to leave even a possible link imperfect. On the day succeeding the fire, I visited the ruins. The walls, with one exception, had fallen in. This exception was found in a compartment wall, not very thick, which stood about the middle of the house, and against which had rested the head of my bed. The plastering had here, in great measure, resisted the action of the fire – a fact which I attributed to its having been recently spread. About this wall a dense crowd were collected, and many persons seemed to be examining a particular portion of it with very minute and eager attention. The words 'strange!' 'singular!' and other similar expressions, excited my curiosity. I approached and saw, as if graven in *bas-relief* upon the white surface, the figure of a gigantic *cat*. The impression was given with an accuracy truly marvellous. There was a rope about the animal's neck.

When I first beheld this apparition – for I could scarcely regard it as less – my wonder and my terror were extreme. But at length reflection came to my aid. The cat, I remembered, had been hung in a garden adjacent to the house. Upon the alarm of fire, this garden had been immediately filled by the crowd – by some one of whom the animal must have been cut from the tree and thrown, through an open window, into my chamber. This had probably been done with the view of arousing me from sleep. The falling of other walls had compressed the victim of my cruelty into the substance of the freshly-spread plaster; the lime of which, with the flames, and the *ammonia* from the carcass, had then accomplished the portraiture as I saw it.

Although I thus readily accounted to my reason, if not altogether to my conscience, for the startling fact just detailed, it did not the less fail to make a deep impression upon my fancy. For months I could not rid myself of the phantasm of the cat; and, during this period, there came back into my spirit a half-sentiment that seemed, but was not, remorse. I went so far as to regret the loss of the animal, and to look about me, among the vile haunts which I now habitually frequented, for another pet of the same species, and of somewhat similar appearance, with which to supply its place.

One night as I sat, half stupefied, in a den of more than infamy, my attention was suddenly drawn to some black object, reposing upon the head of one of the immense hogsheads of gin, or of rum, which constituted the chief furniture of the apartment. I had been looking steadily at the top of this hogshead for some minutes, and what now caused me surprise was the fact that I had not sooner perceived the object thereupon. I approached it, and touched it with my hand. It was a black cat – a very large one – fully as large as Pluto, and closely resembling him in every respect but one. Pluto had not a white hair upon any portion of his body; but this cat had a large, although indefinite splotch of white, covering nearly the whole region of the breast.

Upon my touching him, he immediately arose, purred loudly,

rubbed against my hand, and appeared delighted with my notice.
This, then, was the very creature of which I was in search. I at once
offered to purchase it of the landlord; but this person made no
claim to it – knew nothing of it – had never seen it before.

I continued my caresses, and, when I prepared to go home, the
animal evinced a disposition to accompany me. I permitted it to
do so; occasionally stooping and patting it as I proceeded. When
it reached the house it domesticated itself at once, and became
immediately a great favorite with my wife.

For my own part, I soon found a dislike to it arising within me.
This was just the reverse of what I had anticipated; but – I know
not how or why it was – its evident fondness for myself rather
disgusted and annoyed. By slow degrees, these feelings of disgust
and annoyance rose into the bitterness of hatred. I avoided the
creature; a certain sense of shame, and the remembrance of my
former deed of cruelty, preventing me from physically abusing it. I
did not, for some weeks, strike, or otherwise violently ill use it; but
gradually – very gradually – I came to look upon it with unutterable
loathing, and to flee silently from its odious presence, as from the
breath of a pestilence.

What added, no doubt, to my hatred of the beast, was the
discovery, on the morning after I brought it home, that, like Pluto,
it also had been deprived of one of its eyes. This circumstance,
however, only endeared it to my wife, who, as I have already said,
possessed, in a high degree, that humanity of feeling which had
once been my distinguishing trait, and the source of many of my
simplest and purest pleasures.

With my aversion to this cat, however, its partiality for myself
seemed to increase. It followed my footsteps with a pertinacity
which it would be difficult to make the reader comprehend.
Whenever I sat, it would crouch beneath my chair, or spring upon

my knees, covering me with its loathsome caresses. If I arose to
walk it would get between my feet and thus nearly throw me down,
or, fastening its long and sharp claws in my dress, clamber, in this
manner, to my breast. At such times, although I longed to destroy
it with a blow, I was yet withheld from so doing, partly by a
memory of my former crime, but chiefly — let me confess it at once
— by absolute *dread* of the beast.

This dread was not exactly a dread of physical evil — and yet I
should be at a loss how otherwise to define it. I am almost ashamed
to own — yes, even in this felon's cell, I am almost ashamed to own
— that the terror and horror with which the animal inspired me,
had been heightened by one of the merest chimeras it would be
possible to conceive. My wife had called my attention, more than
once, to the character of the mark of white hair, of which I have
spoken, and which constituted the sole visible difference between
the strange beast and the one I had destroyed. The reader will
remember that this mark, although large, had been originally very
indefinite; but, by slow degrees — degrees nearly imperceptible, and
which for a long time my Reason struggled to reject as fanciful — it
had, at length, assumed a rigorous distinctness of outline. It was
now the representation of an object that I shudder to name — and
for this, above all, I loathed, and dreaded, and would have rid
myself of the monster *had I dared* — it was now, I say, the image of a
hideous — of a ghastly thing — of the GALLOWS! — oh, mournful and
terrible engine of Horror and of Crime — of Agony and of Death!

And now was I indeed wretched beyond the wretchedness
of mere Humanity. And *a brute beast* — whose fellow I had
contemptuously destroyed — *a brute beast* to work out for *me* — for
me a man, fashioned in the image of the High God — so much
of insufferable woe! Alas! neither by day nor by night knew I the
blessing of Rest any more! During the former the creature left me

no moment alone; and, in the latter, I started, hourly, from dreams of unutterable fear, to find the hot breath of *the thing* upon my face, and its vast weight – an incarnate Night-Mare that I had no power to shake off – incumbent eternally upon my *heart!*

Beneath the pressure of torments such as these, the feeble remnant of the good within me succumbed. Evil thoughts became my sole intimates – the darkest and most evil of thoughts. The moodiness of my usual temper increased to hatred of all things and of all mankind; while, from the sudden, frequent and ungovernable outbursts of a fury to which I now blindly abandoned myself, my uncomplaining wife, alas! was the most usual and the most patient of sufferers.

One day she accompanied me, upon some household errand, into the cellar of the old building which our poverty compelled us to inhabit. The cat followed me down the steep stairs, and, nearly throwing me headlong, exasperated me to madness. Uplifting an axe, and forgetting, in my wrath, the childish dread which had hitherto stayed my hand, I aimed a blow at the animal which, of course, would have proved instantly fatal had it descended as I wished. But this blow was arrested by the hand of my wife. Goaded, by the interference, into a rage more than demoniacal, I withdrew my arm from her grasp and buried the axe in her brain. She fell dead upon the spot, without a groan.

This hideous murder accomplished, I set myself forthwith, and with entire deliberation, to the task of concealing the body. I knew that I could not remove it from the house, either by day or by night, without the risk of being observed by the neighbors. Many projects entered my mind. At one period I thought of cutting the corpse into minute fragments, and destroying them by fire. At another, I resolved to dig a grave for it in the floor of the cellar. Again, I deliberated about casting it in the well in the yard – about packing it in a box, as if merchandise, with the usual arrangements, and so getting a porter to take it from the house. Finally I hit upon what I considered a far better expedient than either of these. I determined to wall it up in the cellar – as the monks of the Middle Ages are recorded to have walled up their victims.

For a purpose such as this the cellar was well adapted. Its walls were loosely constructed, and had lately been plastered throughout with a rough plaster, which the dampness of the atmosphere had prevented from hardening. Moreover, in one of the walls was a projection, caused by a false chimney, or fireplace, that had been filled up, and made to resemble the rest of the cellar. I made no doubt that I could readily displace the bricks at this point, insert the corpse and wall the whole up as before, so that no eye could detect any thing suspicious.

And in this calculation I was not deceived. By means of a crowbar I easily dislodged the bricks, and, having carefully deposited the body against the inner wall, I propped it in that position, while, with little trouble, I relaid the whole structure as it originally stood. Having procured mortar, sand and hair, with every possible precaution, I prepared a plaster which could not be distinguished from the old, and with this I very carefully went over the new brick-work. When I had finished, I felt satisfied that all was right. The wall did not present the slightest appearance of having been disturbed. The rubbish on the floor was picked up with the minutest care. I looked around triumphantly, and said to myself – 'Here at least, then, my labor has not been in vain.'

My next step was to look for the beast which had been the cause of so much wretchedness; for I had, at length, firmly resolved to put it to death. Had I been able to meet with it at the moment, there could have been no doubt of its fate; but it appeared that the crafty animal had been alarmed at the violence of my previous anger, and forbore to present itself in my present mood. It is impossible to describe, or to imagine, the deep, the blissful sense of relief which the absence of the detested creature occasioned in my bosom. It did not make its appearance during the night – and thus for one night, at least, since its introduction into the house, I soundly and tranquilly slept; aye, *slept* even with the burden of murder upon my soul!

The second and the third day passed, and still my tormentor came not. Once again I breathed as a freeman. The monster, in terror, had fled the premises forever! I should behold it no more! My happiness was supreme! The guilt of my dark deed disturbed me but little. Some few inquiries had been made, but these had been readily answered. Even a search had been instituted – but of course nothing was to be discovered. I looked upon my future felicity as secured.

Upon the fourth day of the assassination, a party of the police came, very unexpectedly, into the house, and proceeded again to make rigorous investigation of the premises. Secure, however, in the inscrutability of my place of concealment, I felt no embarrassment whatever. The officers bade me accompany them in their search. They left no nook or corner unexplored. At length, for the third or fourth time, they descended into the cellar. I quivered not in a muscle. My heart beat calmly as that of one who slumbers in innocence. I walked the cellar from end to end. I folded my arms upon my bosom, and roamed easily to and fro. The police were thoroughly satisfied and prepared to depart. The glee at my heart was too strong to be restrained. I burned to say if but one word, by way of triumph, and to render doubly sure their assurance of my guiltlessness.

'Gentlemen,' I said at last, as the party ascended the steps, 'I delight to have allayed your suspicions. I wish you all health, and

a little more courtesy. By the bye, gentlemen, this – this is a very
well-constructed house,' (in the rabid desire to say something
easily, I scarcely knew what I uttered at all), – 'I may say an
excellently well-constructed house. These walls – are you going,
gentlemen? – these walls are solidly put together'; and here,
through the mere frenzy of bravado, I rapped heavily, with a cane
which I held in my hand, upon that very portion of the brickwork
behind which stood the corpse of the wife of my bosom.

But may God shield and deliver me from the fangs of the Arch-
Fiend! No sooner had the reverberation of my blows sunk into
silence, than I was answered by a voice from within the tomb! – by
a cry, at first muffled and broken, like the sobbing of a child, and
then quickly swelling into one long, loud and continuous scream,
utterly anomalous and inhuman – a howl – a wailing shriek, half of
horror and half of triumph, such as might have arisen only out of
hell, conjointly from the throats of the damned in their agony and
of the demons that exult in the damnation.

Of my own thoughts it is folly to speak. Swooning, I staggered
to the opposite wall. For one instant the party on the stairs
remained motionless, through extremity of terror and of awe. In
the next, a dozen stout arms were toiling at the wall. It fell bodily.
The corpse, already greatly decayed and clotted with gore, stood
erect before the eyes of the spectators. Upon its head, with red
extended mouth and solitary eye of fire, sat the hideous beast
whose craft had seduced me into murder, and whose informing
voice had consigned me to the hangman. I had walled the monster
up within the tomb!

Oscar Wilde

from 'The Sphinx'

In a dim corner of my room for longer than my fancy thinks
A beautiful and silent Sphinx has watched me through the
    shifting gloom.

Inviolate and immobile she does not rise she does not stir
For silver moons are naught to her and naught to her the suns
    that reel.

Red follows grey across the air, the waves of moonlight ebb and flow
But with the Dawn she does not go and in the night-time
    she is there.

Dawn follows Dawn and Nights grow old and all the while this
    curious cat
Lies couching on the Chinese mat with eyes of satin rimmed
    with gold.

Upon the mat she lies and leers and on the tawny throat of her
Flutters the soft and silky fur or ripples to her pointed ears.

Come forth, my lovely seneschal! so somnolent, so statuesque!
Come forth you exquisite grotesque! half woman and half animal!

Come forth my lovely languorous Sphinx! and put your head upon
    my knee!
And let me stroke your throat and see your body spotted like
    the Lynx!

And let me touch those curving claws of yellow ivory and grasp
The tail that like a monstrous Asp coils round your heavy velvet paws!

A thousand weary centuries are thine while I have hardly seen
Some twenty summers cast their green for Autumn's gaudy liveries.

But you can read the Hieroglyphs on the great sand-stone obelisks,
And you have talked with Basilisks, and you have looked on
    Hippogriffs.

O tell me, were you standing by when Isis to Osiris knelt?
And did you watch the Egyptian melt her union for Antony

And drink the jewel-drunken wine and bend her head in mimic awe
To see the huge proconsul draw the salted tunny from the brine?

And did you mark the Cyprian kiss white Adon on his catafalque?
And did you follow Amenalk, the God of Heliopolis?

And did you talk with Thoth, and did you hear the moon-horned
    Io weep?
And know the painted kings who sleep beneath the wedge-shaped
    Pyramid?

Lift up your large black satin eyes which are like cushions where
    one sinks!
Fawn at my feet, fantastic Sphinx! and sing me all your memories!

William Butler Yeats

The Cat and the Moon

The cat went here and there
And the moon spun round like a top,
And the nearest kin of the moon,
The creeping cat, looked up.
Black Minnaloushe stared at the moon,
For, wander and wail as he would,
The pure cold light in the sky

Troubled his animal blood.
Minnaloushe runs in the grass
Lifting his delicate feet.
Do you dance, Minnaloushe, do you dance?
When two close kindred meet,
What better than call a dance?
Maybe the moon may learn,
Tired of that courtly fashion,
A new dance turn.
Minnaloushe creeps through the grass
From moonlit place to place,
The sacred moon overhead
Has taken a new phase.
Does Minnaloushe know that his pupils
Will pass from change to change,
And that from round to crescent,
From crescent to round they range?
Minnaloushe creeps through the grass
Alone, important and wise,
And lifts to the changing moon
His changing eyes.

Kitten

*For he is an instrument for the children
to learn benevolence upon.*

Christopher Smart

Brian Vesey-Fitzgerald from *Penguin Handbooks: Cats*

The Care and Training of Kittens

A new kitten should be petted as much as possible during its first few days in its new home. It will get to know all about the house of its own accord pretty quickly, but it is even more important that it should get to know about its new owner, and that it cannot do without co-operation. Hold it on your lap and against your shoulder, stroke it (especially its head gently with one finger) and talk to it quietly in a soft voice. The warmth of your body and the sound of your voice will soothe it, and help it to know that you are friendly.

Talking is, I think, particularly important. Talking from the very beginning of your acquaintance helps throughout the cat's life and especially during its training. I have always made a great point of talking to my cats from kittenhood onward, and very soon they have come to know the different tones of my voice. All my cats have talked back to me, and most of them have started to do so almost at once. This initial conversation does make a great difference to the cat's outlook on life.

Lewis Carroll, from *Through the Looking Glass*

An Inconvenient Habit of Kittens

It is a very inconvenient habit of kittens (Alice had once made the remark) that, whatever you say to them, they *always* purr. 'If they would only purr for "yes", and mew for "no", or any rule of that sort,' she had said, 'so that one could keep up a conversation! But how *can* you talk with a person if they *always* say the same thing?'

On this occasion the kitten only purred: and it was impossible to guess whether it meant 'yes' or 'no'.

Lewis Carroll, from *Through the Looking Glass*

The Black Kitten

The way Dinah washed her children's faces was this: first she held the poor thing down by its ear with one paw, and then with the other paw she rubbed its face all over, the wrong way, beginning at the nose: and just now, as I said, she was hard at work on the white kitten, which was lying quite still and trying to purr – no doubt feeling that it was all meant for its good.

But the black kitten had been finished with earlier in the afternoon, and so, while Alice was sitting curled up in a corner of the great arm-chair, half talking to herself and half asleep, the kitten had been having a grand game of romps with the ball of worsted Alice had been trying to wind up, and had been rolling it up and down till it had all come undone again; and there it was, spread over the hearth-rug, all knots and tangles, with the kitten running after its own tail in the middle.

'Oh, you wicked little thing!' cried Alice, catching up the kitten, and giving it a little kiss to make it understand that it was in disgrace. 'Really, Dinah ought to have taught you better manners! You *ought*, Dinah, you know you ought!' she added, looking reproachfully at the old cat, and speaking in as cross a voice as she could manage – and then she scrambled back into the arm-chair, taking the kitten and the worsted with her, and began winding up the ball again. But she didn't get on very fast, as she was talking all the time, sometimes to the kitten, and sometimes to herself. Kitty sat very demurely on her knee, pretending to watch the progress of the winding, and now and then putting out one paw and gently touching the ball, as if it would be glad to help, if it might.

'Do you know what to-morrow is, Kitty?' Alice began. 'You'd have guessed if you'd been up in the window with me – only Dinah was making you tidy, so you couldn't. I was watching the boys getting in sticks for the bonfire – and it wants plenty of sticks, Kitty! Only it got so cold, and it snowed so, they had to leave off. Never mind, Kitty, we'll go and see the bonfire to-morrow.' Here Alice wound two or three turns of the worsted round the kitten's neck, just to see how it would look: this led to a scramble, in which the ball rolled down upon the floor, and yards and yards of it got unwound again.

'Do you know, I was so angry, Kitty,' Alice went on as soon as they were comfortably settled again, 'when I saw all the mischief you had been doing, I was very nearly opening the window, and putting you out into the snow! And you'd have deserved it, you little mischievous darling! What have you got to say for yourself? Now don't interrupt me!' she went on, holding up one finger. 'I'm going to tell you all your faults. Number one: you squeaked twice while Dinah was washing your face this morning. Now you can't deny it, Kitty: I heard you! What's that you say?' (pretending that the kitten was speaking.) 'Her paw went into your eye? Well, that's *your* fault, for keeping your eyes open – if you'd shut them tight up, it wouldn't have happened. Now don't make any more excuses, but listen! Number two: you pulled Snowdrop away by the tail just as I had put down the saucer of milk before her! What, you were thirsty, were you? How do you know she wasn't thirsty too? Now

for number three: you unwound every bit of the worsted while I
wasn't looking!

'That's three faults, Kitty, and you've not been punished for any
of them yet. You know I'm saving up all your punishments for
Wednesday week – Suppose they had saved up all *my* punishments!'
she went on, talking more to herself than the kitten. 'What *would*
they do at the end of a year? I should be sent to prison, I suppose,
when the day came.'

Robertson Davies, from *The Diary of Samuel Marchbanks*

Tiger

SATURDAY

Kitten arrived today – a tortoiseshell inclining toward tiger stripes;
its milk-name was 'Tiger', and it may stick unless I can think of
something better. It is a female, so Nicholas and Solomon must be
abandoned. Cats marked in this way reveal Chinese ancestry, so I
am told, but so far Tiger has shown none of the much-advertised
Chinese calm. She has climbed the curtains, skated on the lid of
the piano and displayed an utterly anti-Confucian passion for fish
scraps, bits of chicken, custard, junket, bread-and-milk and similar
flesh-pots. A stickler for tradition, I wanted to butter her paws
to accustom her to her new home, but the butter price will not
permit it. Engaged in a lively discussion as to whether olive-oil was
a permissible substitute. Made a punching-bag for Tiger out of a
ball of paper and some string, and watched her box; kittens and
babies are always able to reduce us to the last extreme of drooling
fatuity; at last Tiger was settled for the night in a box containing an

old sweater and a hot-water bottle, the latter being a substitute for her mother. I hope she doesn't get a shock in the morning, when she finds her mother has turned cold, bald and a disagreeable shade of red.

TUESDAY

Seriously disappointed in my kitten Tiger today. During the evening a mouse climbed up through a cold-air grating near my chair and surveyed the room with satisfaction. Aha, I thought, and fetched Tiger, who was sleeping elsewhere. I put her down by the grating, but she immediately climbed up on a sofa and went back to sleep. The mouse appeared again, but I made such a noise waking Tiger up that I frightened it away. But Tiger was now disposed to play, so I exercised her with her personal punch-bag for twenty minutes or so. Then the mouse came back. Anticipating a splendid display of jungle ferocity and agility I pointed it out to Tiger, who sat down and looked at it philosophically. Sensing the situation the mouse began to make free of the room and ran about happily, while Tiger watched, and I tore out my hair in double-handfuls. At last, however, this unnatural cat decided to chase the mouse, and bumped her nose on a door just as the mouse dashed under it …
I wonder if Tiger's glands work properly?

FRIDAY

Since I got a cat of my own, my life has been full of cats. Visited a lady today who has two beautiful black and white cats named Inky and Pinky. I hear news occasionally of my brother Fairchild's Persian, named Button Boots. I see cats on the streets and by the roadside, where I never saw a cat before. A few days ago, making my way toward the In and Out shop, I was almost knocked over by a black Persian, as big as a spaniel, dashing past me, pursued by a man carrying a wrapped bottle. Whether it was a jinni which had escaped from the liquor I did not have time to enquire. As for my own kitten Tiger, I am learning things from her that I never knew before. First of all, I never knew that a kitten could burp, which Tiger does with all the abandon of an old mariner. Second, I never realized that a kitten could be completely and infallibly house-trained, and suddenly forget all it had been taught, reverting to intolerable Bohemianism. Also, why does she like to hide in the piano, plucking ghostly music from the strings with her claws? Is she a sphinx, or merely a humorist of a somewhat earthy sort?

WEDNESDAY

Tiger is not better, so I took her to the veterinary this evening. He diagnosed her case as one of garbage-eating; when she ran away she must have treated herself to a bit of over-ripe fish. He gave me some pills for her, and also demonstrated the proper way to give pills to a cat; you suddenly draw the cat's head backward, pry open its mouth, shove the pill down into its stomach with a pair of forceps, and whisk the pill briskly around in its insides. Then you let go, and the cat uses language that scorches its whiskers. I decided that I would use the alternative method, which is to powder the pill and slip it slyly into the cat's food. A man who is accustomed to going right to the seat of the trouble with a sick cow, and giving pills like baseballs to Percheron stallions, may safely take liberties with Tiger, but I am not in his class as a beast-tamer, and I know it. 'A cat is no fool, and she may resent this,' he said: I knew that, too.

Thomas Hood

Choosing their Names

Our old cat has kittens three —
What do you think their names should be?
One is tabby with emerald eyes,
And a tail that's long and slender,
And into a temper she quickly flies
If you ever by chance offend her.
I think we shall call her this —
I think we shall call her that —
Now, don't you fancy 'Pepper-pot'
A nice name for a cat?

One is black with a frill of white,
And her feet are all white fur, too;
If you stroke her she carries her tail upright
And quickly begins to purr, too.
I think we shall call her this —
I think we shall call her that —
Now, don't you fancy 'Sootikin'
A nice name for a cat?

One is tortoise-shell, yellow and black,
With a lot of white about him:
If you tease him, at once he sets up his back:
He's a quarrelsome one, ne'er doubt him!
I think we shall call him this —
I think we shall call him that —

Now, don't you fancy 'Scratchaway'
A nice name for a cat?

Our old cat has kittens three
And I fancy these their names will be:
'Pepper-pot', 'Sootikin', 'Scratchaway' – there!
Were ever kittens with these to compare?
And we call the old mother – now, what do you think?
Tabitha Longclaws Tiddley Wink.

This Strange Affection

My friend had a little helpless leveret brought to him, which the servants fed with milk in a spoon, and about the same time his cat kittened and the young were dispatched and buried. The hare was soon lost, and supposed to have gone the way of most foundlings, to be killed by some dog or cat. However, in about a fortnight, as the master was sitting in his garden in the dusk of the evening, he observed his cat, with tail erect, trotting towards him, and calling with little short inward notes of complacency, such as they use towards their kittens, and something gamboling after, which proved to be the leveret that the cat had supported with her milk, and continued to support with great affection.

Thus was a graminivorous animal nurtured by a carnivorous and predaceous one!

Why so cruel and sanguinary a beast as a cat, of the ferocious genus of *Feles*, the *murium leo*, as Linnaeus calls it, should be affected with any tenderness towards an animal which is its natural prey, is not so easy to determine.

This strange affection probably was occasioned by that *desiderium*, those tender maternal feelings, which the loss of her kittens had awakened in her breast; and by the complacency and ease she derived to herself from the procuring her teats to be drawn, which were too much distended with milk, till, from habit, she became as much delighted with this foundling as if it had been her real offspring.

Beatrix Potter

The Tale of Tom Kitten

Once upon a time there were three little kittens, and their names were – Mittens, Tom Kitten and Moppet. They had dear little fur coats of their own; and they tumbled about the doorstep and played in the dust.

But one day their mother – Mrs Tabitha Twitchit – expected friends to tea; so she fetched the kittens indoors, to wash and dress them, before the fine company arrived.

First she scrubbed their faces (this one is Moppet).

Then she brushed their fur (this one is Mittens).

Then she combed their tails and whiskers (this is Tom Kitten).

Tom was very naughty, and he scratched.

Mrs Tabitha dressed Moppet and Mittens in clean pinafores
and tuckers; and then she took all sorts of elegant uncomfortable
clothes out of a chest of drawers, in order to dress up her son Thomas.

Tom Kitten was very fat, and he had grown; several buttons burst
off. His mother sewed them on again.

When the three kittens were ready, Mrs Tabitha unwisely turned
them out into the garden, to be out of the way while she made hot
buttered toast. 'Now keep your frocks clean, children! You must
walk on your hind legs.'

'Keep away from the dirty ash-pit, and from Sally Henny-penny,
and from the pig-stye and the Puddle-ducks.'

Moppet and Mittens walked down the garden path unsteadily.
Presently they trod upon their pinafores and fell on their noses.
When they stood up there were several green smears!

'Let us climb up the rockery, and sit on the garden wall,' said Moppet. They turned their pinafores back to front, and went up with a skip and a jump; Moppet's white tucker fell down into the road.

Tom Kitten was quite unable to jump when walking upon his hind legs in trousers. He came up the rockery by degrees, breaking the ferns, and shedding buttons right and left.

He was all in pieces when he reached the top of the wall. Moppet and Mittens tried to pull him together; his hat fell off, and the rest of his buttons burst.

While they were in difficulties, there was a pit pat paddle pat! And the three Puddle-ducks came along the hard high road, marching one behind the other and doing the goose step – pit pat paddle pat! Pit pat waddle pat!

They stopped and stood in a row, and stared up at the kittens. They had very small eyes and looked surprised.

Then the two duck-birds, Rebeccah and Jemima Puddle-duck, picked up the hat and tucker and put them on.

Mittens laughed so that she fell off the wall. Moppet and Tom descended after her; the pinafores and all the rest of Tom's clothes came off on the way down. 'Come! Mr Drake Puddle-duck,' said Moppet – 'Come and help us to dress him! Come and button up Tom!'

Mr Drake Puddle-duck advanced in a slow sideways manner, and picked up the various articles.

But he put them on *himself*! They fitted him even worse than Tom Kitten. 'It's a very fine morning!' said Mr Drake Puddle-duck.

And he and Jemima and Rebeccah Puddle-duck set off up the road, keeping step – pit pat, paddle pat! Pit pat, waddle pat!

Then Tabitha Twitchit came down the garden and found her kittens on the wall with no clothes on.

She pulled them off the wall, smacked them and took them back to the house. 'My friends will arrive in a minute, and you are not fit to be seen; I am affronted,' said Mrs Tabitha Twitchit. She sent them upstairs; and I am sorry to say she told her friends that they were in bed with the measles, which was not true.

Quite the contrary; they were not in bed; *not* in the least. Somehow there were very extraordinary noises over-head, which disturbed the dignity and repose of the tea-party.

And I think that some day I shall have to make another, larger, book, to tell you more about Tom Kitten!

As for the Puddle-ducks – they went into a pond. The clothes all came off directly, because there were no buttons.

And Mr Drake Puddle-duck, and Jemima and Rebeccah, have been looking for them ever since.

William Wordsworth

The Kitten and Falling Leaves

That way, look, my Infant, lo!
What a pretty baby-show!
See the kitten on the wall,
Sporting with the leaves that fall.
Withered leaves – one – two – and three
From the lofty elder tree!
Through the calm and frosty air,
Of this morning bright and fair,
Eddying round and round they sink,
Softly, slowly: one might think,
From the motions that are made,

Every little leaf conveyed
Sylph or Faery hither tending, –
To this lower world descending,
Each invisible and mute,
In his wavering parachute.
– But the Kitten, how she starts,
Crouches, stretches, paws and darts!
First at one, and then its fellow,
Just as light and just as yellow;
There are many now – now one –
Now they stop and there are none:
What intenseness of desire
In her upward eye of fire!
With a tiger-leap half-way,
Now she meets the coming prey.
Lets it go as fast, and then
Has it in her power again:
Now she works with three or four,
Like an Indian conjurer;
Quick as he in feats of art,
Far beyond in joy of heart.
Were her antics played in the eye
Of a thousand standers-by,
Clapping hands with shout and stare,
What would little Tabby care
For the plaudits of the crowd?
Over happy to be proud,
Over wealthy in the treasure
Of her own exceeding pleasure!

* * *

Yet, whate'er enjoyments dwell
In the impenetrable cell
Of the silent heart which Nature
Furnishes to every creature;
Whatsoe'er we feel and know
Too sedate for outward show,
Such a light of gladness breaks,
Pretty Kitten! From thy freaks, –
Spreads with such a living grace
O'er my little Dora's face;
Yes, the sight so stirs and charms
Thee, Baby, laughing in my arms,
That almost I could repine
That your transports are not mine,
That I do not wholly fare
Even as ye do, thoughtless pair!
And I will have my careless season
Spite of melancholy reason,
Will walk through life in such a way
That, when time brings on decay,

Now and then I may possess
Hours of perfect gladsomeness.
– Pleased by any random toy;
By a kitten's busy joy,
Or an infant's laughing eye
Sharing in the ecstasy;
I would fare like that or this,
Find my wisdom in my bliss;
Keep the sprightly soul awake,
And have faculties to take,
Even from things by sorrow wrought,
Matter for a jocund thought,
Spite of care, and spite of grief,
To gambol with Life's falling Leaf.

Big Cat

*For the Cherub Cat is a term
of the Angel Tiger.*

Christopher Smart

William Blake

The Tyger

Tyger Tyger, burning bright,
In the forests of the night;
What immortal hand or eye,
Could frame thy fearful symmetry?

In what distant deeps or skies
Burnt the fire of thine eyes?
On what wings dare he aspire?
What the hand dare sieze the fire?

And what shoulder, & what art,
Could twist the sinews of thy heart?
And when thy heart began to beat,
What dread hand? & what dread feet?

What the hammer? what the chain?
In what furnace was thy brain?
What the anvil? what dread grasp
Dare its deadly terrors clasp!

When the stars threw down their spears
And water'd heaven with their tears,
Did he smile his work to see?
Did he who made the Lamb make thee?

Tyger! Tyger! burning bright,
In the forests of the night,
What immortal hand or eye
Dare frame thy fearful symmetry?

William Blake

from 'Proverbs of Hell'

The tygers of wrath are wiser than the horses of instruction.
The wrath of the lion is the wisdom of God.

John Milton, from *Paradise Lost*

Satan's First Sight of Adam and Eve

So hand in hand they passed, the loveliest pair
That ever since in love's embraces met,
Adam the goodliest man of men since born
His sons, the fairest of her daughters Eve.

* * *

… About them frisking played
All beasts of the earth, since wild, and of all chase
In wood or wilderness, forest or den;
Sporting the lion ramped, and in his paw
Dandled the kid; bears, tigers, ounces, pards,
Gambolled before them …

* * *

Down [Satan] alights among the sportful herd
Of those four-footed kinds, himself now one,
Now other, as their shape served best his end
Nearer to view his prey, and unespied

To make what of their state he more might learn
By word or action marked: about them round
A lion now he stalks with fiery glare,
Then as a tiger, who by chance hath spied
In some purlieu two gentle fawns at play,
Straight couches close, then rising changes oft
His couchant watch, as one who chose his ground
Whence rushing he might surest seize them both
Griped in each paw.

The Bible, Book of Daniel 6:16–27

Daniel in the Lions' Den

16 Then the king commanded, and they brought Daniel, and cast
him into the den of lions. Now the king spake and said unto Daniel,
Thy God whom thou servest continually, he will deliver thee.

17 And a stone was brought, and laid upon the mouth of the den;
and the king sealed it with his own signet, and with the signet
of his lords; that the purpose might not be changed concerning
Daniel.

18 Then the king went to his palace, and passed the night fasting:
neither were instruments of musick brought before him: and his
sleep went from him.

19 Then the king arose very early in the morning, and went in haste
unto the den of lions.

²⁰ And when he came to the den, he cried with a lamentable
voice unto Daniel: and the king spake and said to Daniel, O
Daniel, servant of the living God, is thy God, whom thou servest
continually, able to deliver thee from the lions?

²¹ Then said Daniel unto the king, O king, live for ever.

²² My God hath sent his angel, and hath shut the lions' mouths, that
they have not hurt me: forasmuch as before him innocency was
found in me; and also before thee, O king, have I done no hurt.

²³ Then was the king exceedingly glad for him, and commanded that they should take Daniel up out of the den. So Daniel was taken up out of the den, and no manner of hurt was found upon him, because he believed in his God.

²⁴ And the king commanded, and they brought those men which had accused Daniel, and they cast them into the den of lions, them, their children, and their wives; and the lions had the mastery of them, and brake all their bones in pieces or ever they came at the bottom of the den.

²⁵ Then king Darius wrote unto all people, nations, and languages, that dwell in all the earth; Peace be multiplied unto you.

²⁶ I make a decree, That in every dominion of my kingdom men tremble and fear before the God of Daniel: for he is the living God, and steadfast for ever, and his kingdom that which shall not be destroyed, and his dominion shall be even unto the end.

²⁷ He delivereth and rescueth, and he worketh signs and wonders in heaven and in earth, who hath delivered Daniel from the power of the lions.

Edward Fitzgerald (translator)

from *The Rubaiyat of Omar Khayyam, XVII*

They say the Lion and the Lizard keep
The Courts where Jamshyd gloried and drank deep:
And Bahram, that Great Hunter – the Wild Ass
Stamps o'er his Head, and he lies fast asleep.

Erasmus Darwin

Love Riding on the Lion

So playful Love on Ida's flowery sides
With ribbon-rein the indignant lion guides;
Pleased on his brindled back the lyre he rings,
And shakes delirious rapture from the strings;
Slow as the pausing monarch stalks along,
Sheathes his retractile claws, and drinks the song.

Soft nymphs on timid step the triumphs view,
And listening fawns with beating hoofs pursue;
With pointed ears the alarmèd forest starts,
And love and music soften savage hearts.

C. S. Lewis, from *The Lion, The Witch and the Wardrobe*

The Triumph of the Witch

Very quietly the two girls groped their way among the other
sleepers and crept out of the tent. The moonlight was bright
and everything was quite still except for the noise of the river
chattering over the stones. Then Susan suddenly caught Lucy's arm
and said, 'Look!' On the far side of the camping ground, just where
the trees began, they saw the Lion slowly walking away from them
into the wood. Without a word they both followed him.

He led them up the steep slope out of the river valley and then
slightly to the right – apparently by the very same route which

they had used that afternoon in coming from the Hill of the Stone
Table. On and on he led them, into dark shadows and out into pale
moonlight, getting their feet wet with the heavy dew. He looked
somehow different from the Aslan they knew. His tail and his head
hung low and he walked slowly as if he were very, very tired. Then,
when they were crossing a wide open place where there were no
shadows for them to hide in, he stopped and looked round. It was
no good trying to run away so they came towards him. When they
were closer he said,

'Oh, children, children, why are you following me?'

'We couldn't sleep,' said Lucy – and then felt sure that she need
say no more and that Aslan knew what they had been thinking.

'Please, may we come with you – wherever you're going?' said
Susan.

'Well –' said Aslan, and seemed to be thinking. Then he said, 'I
should be glad of company tonight. Yes, you may come, if you will
promise to stop when I tell you, and after that leave me to go on
alone.'

'Oh, thank you, thank you. And we will,'
said the two girls.

Forward they went again and one of the
girls walked on each side of the Lion.
But how slowly he walked! And his
great, royal head
drooped so that his
nose nearly touched
the grass. Presently
he stumbled and
gave a low moan.
'Aslan! Dear
Aslan!' said Lucy,

'what is wrong? Can't you tell us?'

'Are you ill, dear Aslan?' asked Susan.

'No,' said Aslan. 'I am sad and lonely. Lay your hands on my mane so that I can feel that you are there and let us walk like that.'

And so the girls did what they would never have dared to do without his permission, but what they had longed to do ever since they first saw him – buried their cold hands in the beautiful sea of fur and stroked it and, so doing, walked with him. And presently they saw that they were going with him up the slope of the hill on which the Stone Table stood. They went up the side where the trees came furthest up, and when they got to the last tree (it was one that had some bushes about it) Aslan stopped and said,

'Oh, children, children. Here you must stop. And whatever happens, do not let yourselves be seen. Farewell.'

And both the girls cried bitterly (though they hardly knew why) and clung to the Lion and kissed his mane and his nose and his paws and his great, sad eyes. Then he turned from them and walked out on to the top of the hill.

The Brothers Grimm, from *Household Stories*

The Lark and the Lion

There was once a man who had to go on a very long journey, and on his departure he asked his three daughters what he should bring them. The eldest chose pearls, the second diamonds, but the third said, 'Dear father, I wish for a singing soaring lark.' The father promised her she should have it if he could meet with one; and then, kissing all three, he set out.

When the time came round for his return, he had bought the
pearls and diamonds for the two elder sisters, but the lark he had
sought in vain everywhere; and this grieved him very much, for
the youngest daughter was his dearest child. By chance his road
led through a forest, in the middle of which stood a noble castle,
and near that a tree, upon whose topmost bough he saw a singing,
soaring lark. 'Ah! I happen with you in the very nick of time!' he
exclaimed, and bade his servant climb the tree and catch the bird.
But as soon as he stepped up to the tree a Lion sprang from behind,
shaking his mane, and roaring so that the leaves upon the branches
trembled. 'Who will steal my singing, soaring lark?' cried the beast;
'I will eat you up!'

'I did not know,' replied the man, 'that the bird belonged to you;
I will repair the intended injury, and buy myself off with gold; only
let me have my life.'

'Nothing can save you,' said the Lion, 'except you promise me the
first person who meets you on your return home; if you do that, I
will give you not only your life, but also the bird for your daughter.'

This condition the man refused, saying, 'That might be my
youngest daughter, who is dearest to me, and will most likely run
to meet me on my return.' But the servant was anxious, and said, 'It
does not follow that your daughter will come; it may be a cat or a
dog.' At length the man let himself be persuaded, and taking the
singing, soaring lark, he promised the Lion whatever should first
meet him.

Soon he arrived at home, and on entering his house the first who
greeted him was no other than his dearest daughter, who came
running, kissed and embraced him, and when she saw the lark in his
hand was almost beside herself with joy. The poor father, however,
could not rejoice, but began to weep, and said, 'My dearest child,
this bird I have bought very dear; I was forced to promise you for it

to a wild Lion, and when he gets you he will tear you in pieces and eat you.' Then he told her all that had passed, and begged her not to go away, let what might be the consequences. But his daughter consoled him, and said, 'My dear father, what you have promised you must perform; I will go and soften the heart of this Lion, so that I shall soon return to you.'

The next morning she had the way shown to her, and taking leave, she went boldly into the forest. But this Lion was an enchanted prince, who by day, with all his attendants, had the form of lions, and by night they resumed their natural human figure. On her arrival, therefore, the maiden was received kindly, and led into the castle; and when night came on, and the Lion took his natural form, the wedding was celebrated with great splendour. Here they lived contented with each other, sleeping by day and watching by night. One day the Prince said to his wife, 'Tomorrow is a feast day in your father's house, because your eldest sister is to be married, and if you wish to go, my lions shall accompany you.'

She replied that she should very much like to see her father again, and went, accompanied by the lions. On her arrival there was great rejoicing, for all had believed that she had been torn in pieces by the lions, and killed long ago. But she told them what a handsome husband she had, and how well she fared, and stopped with them so long as the wedding lasted; after which she went back into the forest.

Niccolò Macchiavelli

from *The Prince*

There are two ways of fighting: by law or by force. The first way is natural to men, and the second to beasts. But as the first way often proves inadequate one must needs have recourse to the second. So a prince must understand how to make a nice use of the beast and the man … So, as a prince is forced to know how to act like a beast, he must learn from the fox and the lion; because the lion is defenceless against traps and a fox is defenceless against wolves. Therefore one must be a fox in order to recognise traps, and a lion to frighten off wolves. Those who simply act like lions are stupid.

William Blake

from 'Proverbs of Hell'

The fox provides for himself, but God provides for the lion.

In odorem . ps . dd .
eus ds me
us ad te de
luce uigilo.
itiuit in te anima
mea: q multipliciter
tibi caro mea. In t
ra deserta in uia et in
aquosa sic in sancto
apparui tibi: ut uide
rem uirtute tuam et

Arthur Morrison and J. A. Shepherd, from *The Strand Magazine*

Zig Zags at the Zoo

The lion … is a fraud; a posing, theatrical, Turveydrop and Bobadil[4] of a fraud. Look at him in this, his house. He turns up his nose at the visitors and affects a magnanimous superiority. If he were a human being he would wear *pince-nez* and a velvet jacket, and look pityingly great at picture shows, though in his inner heart a mere beer-drinking vulgarian and a smoker of pipes. So always with the lion; he will pose fine and large if he meet you out for a walk in the jungle, and do his utmost to terrify you; if driven to it he may take the liberty of helping himself to a mouthful of you. But all this is only if he has first failed to sneak away unobserved.

* * *

The tiger's superiority to the lion consists chiefly in his candour. He is a wicked, vicious rascal, a thief and a murderer, and he owns it. He doesn't pose. He would always rather run away than be bothered with fighting, unless he happens to be hungry, and so would the lion. But the lion will attitudinize if he thinks you have observed him, and try to make his running away look like magnanimity. The tiger simply bundles off, without any false pride.

---

4   These are fictional characters famous for hypocrisy: Mr Turveydrop is the dancing master in Charles Dicken's *Bleak House*, who 'had everything but any touch of nature'; the braggart Captain Bobadil appears in Ben Jonson's *Every Man in His Humor*.

* * *

We human animals have
long held a conceited
belief that other creatures
shrink and cower under
the gaze of our eyes; and
as example we point to
the big cats. A tiger, we say,
will not look a man in the face.
He won't, but fear is not his motive.
It is superciliousness – a lofty affectation of
indifference, and nothing else. Every cat is
the same in this respect – lion, tiger, leopard,
panther, Tom or tabby. It is only another
expression of the cat's native vanity. Loving to
be stared at and admired, he makes a great show of the most
contemptuous indifference to everybody. Before you reach the
cage you may now and again detect, from the corner of your eye,
the cat observing you with some interest; after you have passed
you may see the same thing – if you are very sly. But while you are
before him, and looking at him, the tiger cuts you dead.

Hilaire Belloc

The Lion

The Lion, the Lion, he dwells in the waste,
He has a big head and a very small waist;
But his shoulders are stark, and his jaws they are grim,
And a good little child will not play with him.

The Tiger

The Tiger, on the other hand, is kittenish and mild,
He makes a pretty playfellow for any little child.
And mothers of large families (who claim to common sense)
Will find a Tiger well repays the trouble and expense.

Index of Authors

List of Illustrations

*For Cloud and Tigerlily:
nearly lightnin' on superintending*

First published in 2015 by
The British Library
96 Euston Road
London NW1 2DB

Richard Adams extract from *Watership Down first published by Rex Collings, reprinted by permission
of David Higham Associates.* **Hilaire Belloc** 'The Lion' and 'The Tiger' from *The Bad Child's Book of
Beasts reprinted by permission of Peters Fraser & Dunlop (www.petersfraserdunlop.com) on behalf of the Estate
of Hilaire Belloc.* **Elizabeth Bishop** 'Lullaby for the Cat' from *The Complete Poems 1927–1979.
UK: published by Jonathan Cape, reprinted by permission of the Random House Group Limited. US:
copyright © 1979, 1983 by Alice Helen Methfessel. Reprinted by permission of Farrar, Straus and Giroux,
LLC.* **Robertson Davies** extracts from *The Diary of Samuel Marchbanks reprinted by permission of
Pendragon Ink.* **Eleanor Farjeon** 'Cats Sleep Anywhere' from *Blackbird Has Spoken, published by
Macmillan, reprinted by permission of David Higham Associates.* **John Gribbin** extract from *In Search
of Schrödinger's Cat published by Transworld, reprinted by permission of David Higham Associates.* **C. S.
Lewis** extract from *The Lion, The Witch and The Wardrobe copyright © C.S. Lewis Pte. Ltd 1950.*
Jaromir Malek reprinted by permission of the author/British Museum Press. **Walter de la
Mare** 'Puss' and 'Five Eyes' courtesy of the Literary Trustees of Walter de la Mare and the
Society of Authors as their representative. **Mervyn Peake** extract from *Titus Groan reprinted by
permission of Peters Fraser & Dunlop (www.petersfraserdunlop.com) on behalf of the Estate of Mervyn Peake.*

Illustrations copyright © 2015 The British Library Board

Cataloguing in Publication Data
A catalogue record for this book is available
from the British Library

ISBN 978 0 7123 5777 7

Designed by Briony Hartley, Goldust Design
Cover by Rawshock Design
Printed in Malta by Gutenberg Press